Ezra's Noh for Willie and Other Plays

FRANCES BENN HALL

MOUNTAIN PRESS

Ezra's Noh for Willie and Other Plays

*For Jim,
Parnell, Terrence and Caitlin*

These plays echo techniques of Yeats' plays for dancers and of Japanese Noh. They bring together dialogue, music, dance and art, but require no "scenery" and are designed to be performed in any bare playing space before a small audience.

The plays all concern literary figures from the past— Hawthorne and Melville, The Brontës, Lord Byron, Phillis Wheatley, Lady Gregory, James Joyce— and, of course, Ezra Pound who introduced Yeats to the Noh in 1913.

TABLE OF CONTENTS

Nathaniel
in Berkshire

NATHANIEL IN BERKSHIRE was first presented in the
Welles Gallery of the Lenox Library on February 28, 1991 with
the following cast:

Japanese Student . . . . Shuichi Sekimoto

Nathaniel Hawthorne . . . . Arthur Collins

Una Hawthorne . . . . Lori Tannenbaum

Hester Prynne . . . . Meeghan Holoway

Herman Melville . . . . David Raskin

Musicians . . . . Shuichi Sekimoto

Jo Wartella

Terrence Hall

Director . . . . Frances Benn Hall

Nathaniel in Berkshire

A one-act play in the Japanese manner

Characters: Nathaniel Hawthorne
Una Hawthorne
Hester Prynne
Herman Melville
Three musicians

(Bare stage. MUSICIANS: *bamboo flute, drone and tabla. Enter DL; the* FIRST MUSICIAN *moves out and addresses the audience; the other two sit DL. When* FIRST MUSICIAN *finishes his introduction he joins them DL.)*

First Musician: Welcome, gentle audience. I am Seami, come from Japan for music study at your beautiful Tanglewood. It is for me a great honor and I work very diligently at my music so that those who brought me will not disappointed. We keep busy all the days and in the evenings we listen to the concerts. Such music! Rising to the stars. It is most exciting and after I cannot sleep.

I come then to this small red cottage and in the practice room, I try to make music that speaks like that I hear on the stage speaking to me. Many evenings I come here. Always it is quiet. But one night it is not the same. One night spirit is here. I am not afraid. In my country we know much of spirits. So I have made for you a play. It is about the spirit that came to the red cottage.

In spirit plays musicians must be sitting here
to play when the spirits dance. Spirits dance
when the feelings are strong. You will see. It
is all as it should be. We can begin.

(He joins other musicians on floor DL. They begin to play. Lights dim to black then up. HAWTHORNE is discovered alone on stage.)

Hawthorne: Why am I here?
Drawn here,
Forced here against my will.
This small red cottage was my home
So short a space of time--
So short a space of country days
That should have been restful
And were not.
Unease.
Yes, the air sings with it.
Unease.
This, a place I fled
And shrink to face again.
Here my thoughts tangle
Like the woods beyond the door.
Tangled woods
That I must fight through
So that I can rest.
Until I level the woods
That tangle my mind,
I cannot rest.

(Una Hawthorne enters DR.   She is wearing a bright red velvet dress and should evoke the child Pearl in The Scarlet Letter.*)*

Una: Father, father, come tell us another story
                          About the bull that raped Europa.

Hawthorne: Child, child,
                          It was a different story I wove for you.
                          There was a sweet cow
                          With garlands of flowers around her neck.

Una: Oh, papa, how you protected us
                          Cleaning up the old myths.
                          Surely you knew we would find out.

Hawthorne: My child, you do not know what you say.

Una: But I do. I always did.
                          You knew how much I understood.
                          You turned me into Pearl!

(Laughing, she exits UL.)

Hawthorne: I did!
                          I made my Una a demon child in a
                              scarlet dress.
                          Sophia would never have let the child
                              wear scarlet.
                          Nor speak the saucy godless words she
                              utters.
                          Una...Pearl....

Cowering behind Dimsdale, I
   fathered you.
Plucked you off a rose bush at the
   prison door.
Tell me, child, is it for that I must pay?
Come back and tell me.
Una, come back! PEARL!

(HESTER PRYNNE, *wearing her scarlet letter, enters R.)*

Hester: Let her go, Nathaniel, she is only running
           To admire herself in the brook.
           And you know you did not come to atone
              for Pearl.
           It was not she drove you from Berkshire.
           You fled the self you encountered
           In the tangled wood.

Hawthorne: Untrue. I met no self.

Hester: You met me.

Hawthorne: You were never myself.
              I conjured you in Salem,
              Draped cloth about a letter
              And gave you a name.

Hester: No, much more.
           You gave me your own dark beauty,
           Your own blue eyes,

Your own lustful heart.

Hawthorne: I deny it. I never lusted.

Hester: But you did. Poor Nathaniel,
Married to your saintly Sophia,
So good, but oh so plain!
No, Nathaniel, when you walked the woods
You were not looking for Sophia
And you sensed me behind every
     bush and tree.

(Music starts. HESTER dances, pantomiming her words and gradually pulling HAWTHORNE into the dance. The FIRST MUSICIAN speaks her lines as she moves.)

First Musician: Poor Nathaniel, sitting day after day
Writing of aged Hepsibah and sweet Phoebe,
Dove plain as Sophia.
How she gloated at being heroine
And never noticed how dull a one she was!
Poor Sophia.
By day you wrote a sad tale of Salem,
But at night when you walked in the
     tangled wood,
I walked with you.
I let down my hair and it bloomed dark
On my shoulders.
And when we came to the brook and
     looked in,
Your own blue eyes looked back at
     you in mine.

(Both are now kneeling DL gazing into imaginary brook. Music stops abruptly and HESTER *takes her own line.)*

Hester: Oh Nathaniel, how you loved
                    brooks and mirrors!

Hawthorne: And pulled away from them.
                (He does so and crosses UR.)
                I admit the itch in the loins was strong here,
                But I put it down,
                Convinced Sophia that three children
                    were enough,
                Slept celibate in our bed.

Hester: And dreamed of me.

Hawthorne: No, Hester,
                Your image gradually paled
                And if I tramped the woods,
                It was resigned to the fact
                That I would never hold you in my arms.
                Nor need to.
                It was not because of you
                That I left Berkshire
                However flattering you would find that.

Hester: Then why did you flee, Nathaniel?

Una: *(appears UL)*
                And why does the minister keep his hand
                    over his heart?
                (disappears UL)

Hester: And why have you returned?

Hawthorne: Something deep within me
               Something left suspended
               Something wrong.

Hester: You wronged no one. You know that.
               But if you were untrue to yourself

               For that you might wear your hand
               Over your heart.
               To be self-true, you might return.

Hawthorne: To be self-true--
               No! I shall never speak of it.
               He burned my letters.
               Would that I had burned his!

Hester: But did not.
               Is it the letters
               So eagerly scanned by scholars
               That grieve you now?
               What sport they have with the letters!
               Almost as much sport as they have with my
                 scarlet one.
               Come, Nathaniel, do not stay and brood.
               Since you are here, come with me
               For one last romp through the tangled wood.

Hawthorne: Go, Hester, and leave me in peace.

Hester:

I leave you, Nathaniel, but not in peace.
Leave you to confront what you fear more
   than me.

(HESTEr exits DL and immediately MELVILLE enters UR.)

Melville:

That I take it would be me.
I suppose I did terrify you, Nathaniel,
In my review of *Mosses*
Evoking those sexual images--
Germinating seeds and all that--
So soon after meeting you
At the picnic on the mountain.
'He shoots his strong New England roots
Into the hot soil of my Southern soul.'
A bit strong, I suppose,
Although that first review was anonymous.
But you never doubted where it came from.
Admit that at least.

Hawthorne:

I suspected , and was appalled.
Sophia was pleased, too innocent
   to understand.

Melville:

But you did. Bravo, Nathaniel.

Hawthorne:

I said I was appalled.
After that I attempted to avoid you.

Melville:

But did not.

Look, I was the younger man,
I was the struggling author.
You had already arrived.
I looked up to you.
And then I met you
In a thunderstorm on a mountain
And realized I loved you.

Of course I pursued you,
The world knows that.
How I begged you again and again
To visit Arrowhead.
And it knows too your lame avoidance.
And when you did come, bringing Una,
Or sitting primly on the piazza
Ready to leap and run.

But now I see you have come round at last.
You have finally come back to tell me
   I was right.
I always knew you would.

Hawthorne: I have come back at last
                    Because I must face you squarely
                    As I shrunk from doing those long years ago.

(MELVILLE *crosses to* HAWTHORNE, *smiling broadly and extending his
hand.)*

Melville: And to take my hand as you should have then,
                    To forgive me for not sensing in you
                    The love you dared not name.

(HAWTHORNE *pushes past him, ignoring the outstretched hand, crosses
UR and turns on him.)*

Hawthorne: I will not take your hand.
Your implying that I have come to do so
Disgusts me as your actions always did.
All those years of our living,
All these years of our dying,
My cowardice has kept me still;
But at last I know I must silence forever,
The lie you fabricated.

I was never drawn to you.
The friendship you tried to force on me
Had mad, sinister implications.
I felt soiled whenever you left my house
And seldom came to yours.
I found you crude, flamboyant,
And I bore our occasional meetings
With dignity and fortitude
When I could not avoid them.
Any sensitive man would have seen
In my excuses not to come to Arrowhead
Polite expressions of my distaste
For your company.
Yet you invited me again and again,
And when I did not come,
You appeared at the door of this red cottage
With some lame excuse or other.
Once you even dressed yourself

As a wooing Spanish cavalier
And galloped up on horseback!

Melville: Come now, you know I always had a flare for
    the drama.

Hawthorne: For melodrama!
I did not want your friendship
Let alone your outlandish love.

And you used me, plucked images from me
To embroider your sea yarns
Until your whale grew to a great white symbol.

Melville: And became my best book. Surely you
    admit that.

Hawthorne: I admit it. It is a great book.
That I would never deny or begrudge.
Or that our talk on the piazza
May have helped it soar beyond
   Omoo or *Typee*.
But I deny that in any way you were a part of
   my life.

But perhaps you won.
Perhaps that is why forgiveness
Comes so hard to my tongue.
You almost assured your winning
With the final affront--

Dedicating *Moby Dick* to me.
Oh, I grant you, given your bent,
You meant a compliment
But it was self-serving too.
That act made sure our names
Were forever linked.

I was ever polite.
I wrote you a tepid thank you,
So bland and bluff you destroyed it.
But that simple letter of mine
Provoked the famous Farewell Letter
With its deluge of slime
My lips even now cannot utter.

(The MUSICIANS *quote lines from the farewell letter.* MELVILLE *moves toward* HAWTHORNE *who retreats; music under; semi-dance movement.)*

Musician I: By what right do you drink from my flagon of life; and when I put it to my lips--lo, they are yours, not mine.

Musician II: Once you hugged the ugly Socrates because you saw the flame in the mouth and heard the rushing of the demon--and recognized the sound for you have heard it in your solitude.

Musician III: The divine magnet is on you, and my magnet responds, which is the biggest? A foolish question. They are one.

Melville: I admit, extravagantly sexual. But,
             Hawthorne, you understood the prevailing
             thought that impelled the book.

Hawthorne: I understood the prevailing thought of the
             letter well enough and was appalled. I flung
             it from me as though it burned my hand.
             How could I know that Sophia in her
             innocence, would think it should be
             preserved? And now that infamous letter is as
             well-known as Hester's scarlet one. My sin
             was only that in my haste to flee, to put the
             length of the state between us, I did not make
             sure that letter was destroyed.

Melville: You make too much of it. It was euphoric.
             Was it really because of that letter that you
             fled?

Hawthorne: I did not make too much of it.
             But the world has.
             I should have confronted you then,
             But coward still, I fled.

             As we drove through the sleet
             Of that November night
             To board the train in Pittsfield
             Because it seemed unbearable
             That we spend another night in Berkshire,
             I vowed in my heart

That I would never forgive you.
Even now that forgiveness comes hard.
And yet I must forgive.
Must.

I realize now that you were a man
Driven by furies you could not control.
That fate flung us together, I regret.
That our names are forever linked, I rue
But cannot alter.
At last I know and must accept that.
It is too late to stop the scurrying scholars.
They will believe what they choose to believe
And the more titillating the better.

But I know and in your heart you know too
How minuscule was any link between us.
As they ponder, let the scholars remember
That our names are in the same book
Because you put them there.
And let them know most of all
That the answer to all their searching
Is the one word I should have shouted
  long ago
And shout now.
No, Herman Melville, no, no, no!

Melville: (*Stretches out a hand in one last appeal.*)

Hawthorne: (*quietly*) No.

Melville: *(Stares at* HAWTHORNE *a long moment then exits.)*

Hawthorne: *(Stands alone, at peace, taller, as though relieved of a great burden.)*

*(*UNA *and* HESTER *enter UL and DL respectively.)*

Una: Look, mother, the minister no longer has his hand over his heart.

Hester: Hush, child, he is about to take you in his arms.

(One moment quiet tableaux; no one moves. Then blackout; music up.)

Emily's Play

EMILY'S PLAY was first presented in the Lenox Library on March 10, 1992 with the following cast:

Branwell Brontë . . . . Michael Marlow
Emily Brontë . . . . Jennifer Johanos
Woman from UCLA . . . . Diane Prusha
Boy . . . . David Ethredge
Girl . . . . Julia Corby
Musicians
  Celtic Harp . . . . Christine Tulis
  Narrator . . . . David Raskin
  Flute . . . . Carolyn Corby
Direction . . . . Frances Benn Hall

Emily's Play

Characters:	Branwell Brontë
	Emily Brontë
	Woman from UCLA
	Boy
	Girl
	Three musicians
	Celtic harp, flute, drum

*The setting is "in the mind's eye" evoked by the musicians. It is
Penistone Crag overlooking the little town of Haworth. A cloth draped
box or two (rocks to sit on). If stage should have levels, they could be
used to advantage as could stage lights for mood but neither are
necessary. Play designed ideally for small audience in any playing
space.*

*(Blackout. Lights up. MUSICIANS enter L. Ceremony of unfolding and
folding cloth of heatherish purple blue.)*

Musician I: 'High waving heather 'neath stormy
     blasts bending
Midnight and moonlight and bright
     shining stars.
Darkness and glory rejoicingly blending
Earth rising to heaven and
     heaven descending
Man's spirit away from its drear
     dungeon sending
Bursting the fetters and breaking the bars.'

*(MUSICIANS move L and two sit weaving soft background music for voice
of FIRST MUSICIAN.)*

Musician I: High waving heather ripples in the sun.
               Here on the crag we look down over
                 the heather
               Watch the little town fill up with
                 tour busses
               Watch the people move up the steep
                 cobbled streets
               Wander into the parsonage, the graveyard,
                 the church,
               Shaking their heads sadly at the names
                 and dates
               Carved on the stone. Then brightening
               As they move to the gift shop
               For postcards, Brontë tote bags and tea.
               Few find time to wander in the heather.
               None find time to scale the crag.
               We are safe here with memories.

Musician II: You are wrong. One comes.

Musician I: Oh, he. He often comes.
               But see, the wind blows through him
               And his feet dislodge no pebble.

Musician II: Why does he come?

Musician I: We do not know. We think to brood.
               To wait for one who never comes.
               Let him be. He cannot harm us.
               He can no longer harm anyone.

(BRANWELL enters R. He is in the prime of manhood, not the emaciated invalid he eventually became. He sits on a rock and gazes moodily down on the town. The MUSICIANS *regard him, shrug, and begin to play softly. Then* EMILY, *young and vibrant, enters R.* BRANWELL *springs up when she enters.)*

Branwell: You finally came!

Emily: Yes, I knew I'd find you here.

Branwell: Then why did you wait so many years?
I have come again and again,
Watched the scene below change from
   pastoral to circus
Why must they flock here?

Emily: Because we're famous, I suppose.

Branwell: You may be. I'm infamous at best.

Emily: You helped paint that picture, I'm afraid.

Branwell: Painting. Just another of the arts I failed at.
Remember the canvas I painted of us all?
You, Charlotte, Anne and me.
Later I painted me out, but it did no good.
The tourists buy copies of that painting--
Reduced to a postcard--
Your three faces staring out
And a brown blur where my face
   used to be.

Emily:	As you point out, it was you Who took your face from the picture.
Branwell:	I did, didn't I? And so I survive in darkness Wastrel brother of three geniuses. Oh, Emily, why did it happen? I wanted fame so much, and I had talent. Surely I had talent. Say it! Say it!
Emily:	*(patiently)* Yes, Branwell, you had talent.
Branwell:	Then what happened?
Emily:	You squandered it. We all had talent. It must have been in our Irish/Cornish genes. Talented all, and dead so soon. Except for Charlotte, determined to outlive us.
Branwell:	And jolly well did!
Emily:	Yes, poor Charlotte, Even at that, she did not live long. But one did not have to, to outlive us.
Branwell:	But she got it all. The fame. The praise.
Emily:	And it terrified her.

Branwell: It would not have terrified me.
               I would have gloried in it.
               Gone to tea with Thackeray,
               Snubbed Mrs Gaskell.
               Charlotte did not enjoy her fame.

Emily: No, Charlotte did not let herself enjoy much.
               And finally settled for less than second best,
               And could not stomach it,
               Literally could not stomach marriage to
                 tame Arthur,
               Could not accept that within her body
               She carried his seed.
               Poor Charlotte. She really had so little.
               Hopeless love for that aging teacher.
               Not much of a life, ever.

Branwell: She never comes here.

Emily: No, she wouldn't want to.

Branwell: But you came. Finally.

Emily: Yes. Finally. There seemed a need.
               Unfinished business.
               There is something I may tell you.
               Or may not.
               Anyway, I came.
               And I find it all sad,
               All these people, and the busses.

But at least we are safe from them.
They are too fat and lazy to climb here.

Branwell: Once someone did, years ago that was.
But I hid until he went away.
Do you think they could see us?
I mean if someone did come?

Emily: I'm not sure. Maybe if they believed enough.

Branwell: Believed what?

Emily: That we're here.

Branwell: Then I'm taking no chances.
A most awesome looking woman is toiling
   up the rocks.
I'll slip behind the crag until she goes away.

Emily: And I shall stay right where I am
And see if she can see me.
Oh, dear, she looks dreadful.
She doesn't deserve to see me.

(An imposing and rather daunting matron in clam-digger pants and a straw hat heaves into view R. She plops down on a rock and wipes her face with her scarf. She is concerned with getting her breath and does not at first notice EMILY. *When she does, she beams.)*

Woman: Hello. Didn't see you at first. Too busy
catching my breath. Probably a fool to
attempt the climb, but I've just loved the

Brontës for years. I teach a seminar on them at UCLA, and I couldn't go back to California without climbing Cathy's crag, could I?

(She rattles on, evidently a talker who expects few replies.)

My husband is down in the tearoom. He hates this trip so far. He's a golfer and can't wait to get to Scotland and play St. Andrews, but of course being in the arts, I just love it. We're going to Windemere tonight and tomorrow we see Wordsworth's cottage. It's really a wonderful literary experience, I mean just being here. Don't you feel it? The very air seems to sing 'Heathcliff'. I'm sensitive to such things, of course. And it's all so sad down there in the church. I cried. All those pitiful names and dates on the stone. So talented and such short lives. Of course, Charlotte did live a bit longer than the rest. TB carried the others off, but Charlotte died of complications of pregnancy. Oh, I know my Brontë history! So sad, all that genius just cut off.

Emily: *(Suddenly, almost impishly; can we believe her?)*
Maybe it wasn't.

Woman: What do you mean?

Emily: Well, I have my own theories about the
           Brontës, especially about Emily, the sister
           who baffles the critics. How could virginal
           Emily, living the sheltered life she seems to
           have lived, have ever known the passion that
           created Heathcliff?

           I think it possible that Emily had more
           experience than we know, and that she hints
           at it in *Wuthering Heights*. But we can't
           know, will never know, who Heathcliff really
           was.
           (Pause. A real pull-in and she knows it.)
           Or what happened to Emily's child.

Woman: Her child! You're mixed up. Emily had no
           child.

Emily: But she must have had one. His child. As she
           hints in the book. She makes Cathy die,
           having hinted that her child may be
           Heathcliff's. She punishes Cathy for the child
           as she needed to punish herself-- for the child
           she abandoned in Brussels.

Woman: Brussels! You must be mad. You're making
           this up.

Emily: Oh, I think not. Why did Emily, such a
           homebody, leave the moors when she was 24

and go off to Brussels with Charlotte? And she was gone long enough to bear a child, gone the longest time she ever spent away from Haworth.

Woman: But others would have known. Charlotte...people at the school.

Emily: No one need have known. Emily was slight. Her body tightly bound need have shown no signs. It could have happened. Perhaps she was alone when the baby came and told no one. Perhaps Charlotte knew.

I can imagine how it might have been. Emily has gone for a long walk and is caught in a storm. She seeks refuge in an empty church, bears her child in the sacristy, wraps it in an altar cloth and leaves it by the baptismal fount.

Woman: That's nothing but a flight of fancy. You should be a writer yourself. You aren't by chance a Brontë descendant?

Emily: Indeed not. As you have just been bemoaning, there are no Brontë descendants. The line died out with Charlotte and her unborn child. There will never be another Brontë.

Woman: But your yarn...you made it rather
              convincing. Fantastic, of course, but half way
              convincing.

Emily: Just a theory. We all like to spin yarns about
              the Brontës. Their lives ask for it. No. No
              more Brontës.

Woman: A pity. Such a gifted family.

Emily: But not a happy one. It's probably just as
              well.

Woman: Still, such genius. Who could tell what such a
              child might have become?

Emily: Sheer fantasy as you say.

Woman: Heavens! Look how dark the sky is getting.
              I must get back to the bus. Do you want to
              walk down with me?

Emily: No. I came another way and must return the
              way I came. But I'm perfectly safe. My
              brother is about somewhere. He just went
              over that hillock to get me some heather. I
              want to take it back...to where I came from.

Woman: That would be?

Emily: *(evading)*
                  A beautiful place, but alas, no heather. Well,
                  it's been interesting talking to you, but you
                  better hurry and catch your bus. Thank you
                  for letting me spin my yarns. Sometimes I
                  think spirits of the Brontës must haunt this
                  crag and turn us all into romantics.

Woman: Well, it's been fascinating. *(exits R)*
                  *(EMILY stands alone. Music up and EMILY begins swaying dance of
                  rocking a baby in her arms. Halts the dance abruptly as BRANWELL
                  enters.)*

Branwell: I heard.

Emily: *(lightly)*
                  I thought you might.
                  Great fun spinning yarns for gullible tourists.

Branwell: Emily, how could you!

Emily: What?

Branwell: Besmirch your own memory like that.
                  It's bad enough that I have to go down as
                      a wastrel.

Emily: Deserved, Branwell, deserved. We've been
                      over that.

Branwell: Quite. Deserved. Poof, I just threw it away.

Very well, let them so remember me.
But you're different, Emily,
You're the golden girl,
The lonely legend of Haworth.
That woman was a digging scholar.
She'll go back to California
And read that fiction you just wove
Into her next paper on *Wuthering Heights*.

Emily: Has it never occurred to you, Branwell,
                That some of it might be true?

Branwell: You don't mean that.
                You made it up for a lark.
                You made it all up!
                Emily, admit you made it up!!
                (He grabs her and shakes her roughly.)

Emily: *(taunting)*
                Ah, that excites you.
                Cuts close to the bone, doesn't it?

Branwell: *(releasing her)*
                I don't know what you mean.

Emily: Because you've chosen to forget.
                Or to pretend you have.
                You had been drinking that night, Branwell,
                But you were not drunk.
                You remember that night

The night before Charlotte and I left
    for Brussels.

I didn't want to go but Charlotte was firm.
We must get an education and start a school.
Even Papa agreed.
By then I think he had given up on you.

(BRANWELL *sits L with his head in his hands, listening to this, but not wanting to.* EMILY *stands R looking out over the valley, her back to* BRANWELL *as she continues reliving that night.)*

Emily: It was past sunset but there was to be a
                    full moon
                And I was not afraid, Branwell,
                To walk alone on the moor
                To say goodbye to all I loved here.
                It was February, but not too cold,
                And my shawl was warm.
                I hadn't intended to go far,
                But I kept walking
                And though light left the sky
                I knew if I went a bit higher
                I could see the moon coming up.
                So I made my way through the heather.
                All dry with winter
                And a bit higher....

Branwell: DON'T!

Emily: *(firmly)*
                I came upon you.

Branwell: Don't! For God's sake don't go on.

Emily: I came upon you.
                I'll skip details and only state flatly
                That you raped me
                And ran away.
                And when I stopped crying,
                I made my way home and crept into bed
                And lay awake all night.
                And in the morning Charlotte and I left
                   for Brussels.

                I was very naive, Branwell, for all my years.
                It was months before I realized I was
                   pregnant.
                I needed desperately to tell some one,
                Most of all Charlotte, and I couldn't.
                So I kept on, day to day,
                Doing the French lessons, learning
                   embroidery
                And hoping it was all a bad dream.
                And the time went by and no one seemed
                   to notice.
                I was thin and rangy and clothes
                   were loose.

                In the end, Charlotte found out.
                Not that it was you.
                I never told her that.
                Said I'd been attacked on the moor,

That it was too dark to see his face.
She could believe that.
The truth would have killed her.
And she kept the secret. Took it to her grave.
But she had to know, Branwell,
Because she was with me
When the baby came.

It was a weekend and Charlotte and I
Had walked out to the Protestant Cemetery
With flowers for Martha Taylor's grave.
And on the way back the sky suddenly
   grew black
And we knew a great storm was coming.
It did. Fast.
We ran.
The rain pelted us and there was lightning.
Scarlet flashes that lit up the world.
And Charlotte kept urging me to run faster,
And then, in one of the flashes,
We saw a barn and Charlotte dragged me in.
It was then that the pain started
And the baby came.

Charlotte was horrified, but she knew what
   to do.
She cut the cord with the tiny pen knife,
The one father brought her from Liverpool,
And she took off one of her petticoats
To wrap the baby in.

She was really quite wonderful, Branwell,
Brisk, efficient, and deadly calm.

She put the baby in my arms
And I lay there propped against a bale of hay
And the rain beat down on the roof.
We didn't talk,
Just sat there listening to the rain.
I was too tired to think.
But Charlotte's mind was racing.
And when the rain stopped she asked me
If I felt strong enough to walk.
The first words she spoke to me!
Not, 'Whose is it?'
Or, 'How could you!'
But, 'Do you feel strong enough to walk?'
And I said yes and so we walked out
   into the night
And just walked, not talking,
Until we came to a small chapel--
In that Catholic country
There are a lot of little roadside chapels
And they are never locked.
Charlotte led me in
And told me to put the baby down
On the steps in front of the altar
So the priest would find it
When he came in the morning to say Mass.
So I did.
I did what Charlotte told me to do.

Just put the little bundle
Wrapped in Charlotte's flannel petticoat
Down and walked out of the chapel
Without looking back.

We went on to the school
And on the way we talked a little.
I told her about the man on the moor,
But she didn't really want to listen.
She just insisted no one must ever know,
And that we must forget it ever happened.

And when we reached the school,
Once they saw we were safe,
All was confusion because word had come
That Aunt Branwell was dying.
We had to pack at once
And set out for home that night.
On the boat, I stayed below in the cabin.
I bled a lot and threw the bloody rags into
    the sea.

Aunt Branwell was dead before we
    reached home
And it was months before Charlotte
    went back.
By then any talk of the abandoned baby
    was over.
Charlotte would not have dared

To bring up the subject, nor would have
   wanted to.
So we never heard what happened.
But I still wonder, Branwell,
What did happen to that little baby.
It was as though we had buried it
In that churchyard.

And Charlotte never spoke of it again.
Only later, when I wrote *Wuthering Heights*
I think Charlotte felt
That the harshness of Heathcliff
Was my way of punishing the man
   on the moor.
She hated the book, felt she must apologize
To the literary world for its coarseness.
Poor, Charlotte.

Branwell: I can't believe you. I don't want to
   believe you.
And that night I didn't rape you.
No. No. It was not that way.
I was desperate. Unhappy and desperate.
Remember, Emily, remember how close
   we grew
After Charlotte went off as governess.

She and I had been partners
Weaving our Angria stories,
But with her gone, you and I

became comrades
And wove our own stories.
Remember, Emily, remember what we were
  to each other,
Lost children who had only each other.
And then Charlotte returned
With her plans to take you to Brussels.

I remember that night. Of course, I do.
How could I forget?
You and Charlotte were to leave in
  the morning.
Take the coach to London, then sail
  for Brussels.
And I could not bear it.
I left the house that afternoon.

Emily: I remember. You were not there for supper.
Papa was angry
And I was afraid you had gone off drinking
And I would not get to tell you goodbye.

Branwell: So when you walked the moors that night
You were looking for me?

Emily: Perhaps, Branwell, perhaps I was.

Branwell: And found me miserable and alone
And took me in your arms.

*(MUSICIANS, male and female, now take up lines for BRANWELL and EMILY
as the latter two "dance" the rape from Branwell's point of view. Soft
flute accompaniment.)*

Musician II: *(as Emily)*
                    Both of us were crying.

Musician I: *(as Branwell)*
                    And we just stood there
                    Holding each other for a long time.

Musician II: Yes.

Musician I: And when I lowered you to the ground,
                        Emily,
                    It was not rape...but love, Emily.
                        Love. Love.

Musician II: But I don't want it to happen, Branwell,
                    I am trying to push you away.

Musician I: Remember, Emily, remember.
                    It was not like that.
                    You did not push me away.
                    And afterwards, Emily,
                    Because you have chosen to remember
                        it wrong--
                    Afterwards we lay in each other's arms
                    For a long time and stared at the sky.
                    Afterwards I did not run away.

Emily: Perhaps your remembering, my remembering
            Are very different.
            (She rises; deliberately breaking mood.)
            And I was the one who paid.

Branwell: *(rises)*
            Then your story, the baby, wasn't fiction?

Emily: Perhaps not.

Branwell: My God, Emily, don't toy with me.
            I have to know if it was true.

Emily: *(stands silent)*

Branwell: Then perhaps it was.
            Perhaps that is why when you came back
            All was changed.
            You were cold and distant
            And watched me slide from bad to worse
            With a lofty disdain I could not understand.
            Even at the end, Emily,
            When I was dying
            You would not come to my room and
                hold my hand.
            You were in the house and would not
                come to me.

Emily: No, Branwell, the day you were dying
            I went out walking on the moors.
            I could not stay in the house.

I did not come to you then.
But I followed you into death rather swiftly.

Branwell: But first you punished me.
Made me into Heathcliff.

Emily: *(softly)* Yes.

Branwell: Don't punish me still, Emily.
Tell me at least how much of this is true.

Emily: I'm good at fiction, Branwell. It's my forte.
You must decide.

Branwell: Emily...please....

Emily: *(matter-of factly)*
The tour busses have ruined this spot.
I shall not come again.

Branwell: And you won't tell me, ever?

Emily: No.

Branwell: *(Stands silent a moment, then turns angrily and starts off R.)*

Emily: *(suddenly)*
Branwell, wait.

Branwell: *(Stops. The distance of the stage is between them.)*

Emily: It was a little boy.
            I left a note.
            Asked them to name him Patrick.

Branwell: *(bitterly)*
            New added fiction!
            How can that be true?
            That cozy sentimental detail
            Was not a part of the various versions of
              the story
            I've heard you tell today.
            The Patrick note is a bit too much.
            You just invented it.

Emily: Perhaps I did.
            Or should have remembered to include
              it earlier.
            Faulty fiction.
            You were always my severest critic, Branwell.

            Let us go.
            Now you have something more to brood on
            If you insist on returning here.
            As for me, I shall never come here again.
            I prefer the moor of my memory
            To what the world has made of it.

            Come, give me your hand.
            We shall walk down the hill together
              one last time.

Branwell: *(She crosses to him and stands looking up at him. Long pause. She puts out her hand. He takes it. They move off R together. Music up. Play a little.)*

Musician I: And now all is still.
The busses have pulled away.
The sun sinks. Night comes.

Musician II: 'The night is darkening round me
The wild winds coldly blow;
But a tyrant spell has bound me
And I cannot, cannot go.'
She wrote that.

Musician I: I know.

Musician II: But she went. She's gone.
And we, we seem to be captive here. Why?

Musician I: I do not know.
Something brought us here and holds us here.
Perhaps there is more.

Musician II: More what?

Musician I: To the story.
Yes, I hear footsteps on the path.
No spirits these. They laugh and pant.

Musician II: But where do they come from?
The busses are long gone.

Musician I: Hush, they are here.

(BOY AND GIRL, *college age, come panting up, carrying knapsacks. They fling them down on the rock and collapse beside them.*)

Boy: That's quite a climb. And I thought I was in shape!

Girl: So you're not Heathcliff; they climbed a bit more in those days.

Boy: *(standing)*
But I'm here! On Penistone Crag.

Girl: *(sitting up)*
You know we missed the bus.

Boy: I noticed. We'll hitch or make do some way. Do you mind?

Girl: Not at all. I wanted to come up here. It was why I came to Haworth, really. I'm not studying the Brontës or anything. I just love them.

Boy: Right. I had you spotted on the bus. Not just here for the postcards. Just to breathe the Brontë air. Me, too. Standing up here I can pretend I'm Heathcliff or a Brontë. Does that sound crazy to you?.

Girl: Well, you can't be a Brontë. They all died childless. End of the line.

Boy: I know. Here I stand, Jewish boy from Hoboken and almost feel like a Brontë. Pretty dumb.

Girl: You're Jewish?

Boy: Sure. Why does that surprise you?

Girl: No reason. It's just that I thought you said your name was Patrick. Odd for a Jew. Patrick.

Boy: Oh that, blot on the escutcheon. My great-grandfather was a foundling. Came from some place on the continent. Seems there was a note with the baby asking that he be named Patrick so he was. Don't rightly know the whole story or if there is more of it than that, but we've had a Patrick in every generation since.

Girl: Patrick is at least a Brontë name. That's nice.

Boy: Sure. And there are thousands of Patricks in this world. Though I grant you most of them are in Ireland or Boston, and at the moment I am the only one standing on a Brontë hilltop.

Girl: Now that you've done it, are you ready to go down again? It'll be dark soon and though Cathy and Heathcliff were probably sure-footed as mountain goats, I know I'm not.

Boy: Yes, let's go.

(They start off R down the path; their voices come back to us.)

Girl: Patrick, are you a writer?

Boy: Not much of a one yet, but I have hopes.

Girl: Maybe you'll be a genius and I can say I once met you on a hilltop.

Boy: And that could turn into fiction too.

(They are gone. Silence.)

Musician I: I think we can go now.
                 It is quite played out.

Musician II: But...but is it true?

Musician I: Is what true?

Musician II: What they said. Any of them. All of them.

Musician I: Who knows?

Musician II:	You mean nobody knows?
Musician I:	Does it matter?
Musician II:	No. But I think we should know.
Musician I:	Why?
Musician II:	Well, it is our play.
Musician I:	We only thought so. It was Emily's play And now it is over. Let us fold the cloth.
Musician II:	Yes, let us fold the cloth

(ritual of the cloth)

Musician I:	'Cold in the earth--and the deep snow piled above thee Far, far removed, cold in the dreary grave Have I forgot, my only love to love thee, Severed at last by Time's all severing wave.'

(Having folded the cloth they move L. The flutist takes up his flute and begins to play as lights dim. Plays into darkness, then stops and all is still.)

Production note: In March l992 performances in Berkshires the following changes were made in the activity of the musicians:

FIRST MUSICIAN, *Celtic harp, entered, crossed left and began to play.* MUSICIANS *2 and 3 entered R, movingly slowly, almost dance.* MUSICIAN 2 *carried the noh cloth, nine feet long folded over her arm. These two crossed R, outside stage area and ritualistically opened the cloth, starting from center and unfolding out to two sides, like a Japanese fan. They hung the cloth there where it stayed for the whole performance serving somewhat like the hashigakari in Noh ...as a path down which actors entered and exited. Once cloth hung,* MUSICIAN 2 *joined the harpist DL and musician l moved to stage to take Brontë poem lines and play proceeded. At end of play this was all reversed with* MUSICIANS *2 and 3 folding cloth, taking stage where the final Brontë lines were spoken to harp accompaniment, then exiting R and blackout.*

Cloth was 9 feet by 48 inches, painted on canvas...colors mainly purples, heathers, rose etc...stones, heather, lakes etc..impressionistic rather than realistic and in no way "scenery" but rather an other art introduced into the program.

Dance of
the Eland

DANCE OF THE ELAND was first presented as a staged reading, under the title of *Protective Coloration* at Berkshire Community College, Pittsfield, MA. On February 4, 1993 with the following cast:

Night- watchman . . . . William Corby
Phillis Wheatley . . . . Mary Jane Fromm
Nathaniel (also Mask 1) . . . . Don Herold
Susannah (also Mask 2) . . . . Nancy Travis
Mary (also Mask 3) . . . . Anne Guertin

This play was supported by a National Endowment of the Arts Grant for a three week Puritan Seminar at the College led by John Demos of Yale. The play was a project that grew out of the seminar.

Dance of the Eland

Characters: Night Watchman
                   Phillis
                   Mask I, also Nathaniel
                   Mask II, also Susannah
                   Mask III, also Mary

(Darkness. African music, mainly percussion with perhaps an African chant. Music fades as a light appears UR. It comes from a powerful flashlight in the hand of the WATCHMAN *who shines it on the faces of three great carved African masks. We do not see the bodies of the actors, only the grotesquely beautiful faces. Absolute silence.* WATCHMAN *moves about illuminating each face.)*

Watchman: Am I dreaming?
                   I swear to God I heard music.
                   Yet no one is here.
                   Just these crazy masks.
                   I'll be glad when this exhibit
                   Goes back to Africa
                   Or wherever it came from,
                   And the college puts up
                   Something else to edify the students.
                   Something calm and restrained
                   Like Puritans, maybe,
                   Confined. Defined.
                   All worked out neatly by God.
                   An easy to follow pattern
                   Chalked on the soul.

(Sound of a rustle in the darkness.)

Who's there? I heard you.
There's someone in this room.

(Shines lamp around revealing no one.)

I must be going crazy.
I swear I heard something
Yet no one here
Only these awful masks.

Well, I've done my duty.
Back to my post
And dreaming of a better job
Than night watchman.

(He exits. Total darkness. Total silence. Then the lights come up revealing a small slight woman standing DL. She is black, but dressed as a Puritan and wears a white face mask. She comes forward and examines the masks, studies them a long time, then shakes her head.)

Phillis: Why am I here?
I have lain these 200 years quiet
In that white paradise they promised me.
What could bring me this night
To this strange room
And these strange faces?
I clearly do not belong in this place.
(She rushes to door, raps on it politely.)
Young man,
You who were just here.
Return and let me out.
There has been some mistake.

Clearly, some mistake.
I do not belong here.
Perhaps I was to return
To some different room.
Surely not this one.
Here there is nothing I understand.
Young man! Young man!
Open this door.
Open this door immediately!
Perhaps you do not know who I am.
I have, in my time, been respected
And in your time too.
A poet, a published poet
Writing at a time when few women wrote
When few women could write.
Surely that should earn me some respect
Instead of the silly chance that has locked
   me here.
Let me out!
Well, I shall just have to wait , with dignity,
Until he returns, but I can at least
Turn my back on these hideous faces.

(She sits with her back to the masks. They strip the burlap that hung from their chins to their feet--velcro--and let it drop to the floor revealing Puritan dress. They remove their African masks, revealing the white faces of two women and a young man. PHILLIS sits with her back to them, facing front, and sees none of this.)

Susannah: Phillis...

Phillis: Who called my name?

Susannah: Your mistress.

Phillis: *(Turns and recognizes them.)*
                Oh, you are here!
                How glad I am to see you.
                I thought there was a mistake.
                Now I belong again.

Susannah: Belong is perhaps
                Not the right word, Phillis.
                You do not belong.
                Rather, you once belonged to me.
                I purchased you.
                But I did free you before I died
                So you do not belong to any of us.
                And as for belonging to our world,
                No, you cannot claim that.
                You never belonged.
                You understand that, surely.

Phillis: But you were kind to me.
                Taught me to read and write,
                Gave me your God.

Mary: I taught you to read, Phillis,
                Though you soon outstripped me.
                And your poetic gift surprised us.

Susannah: Not unhappily, of course.
                Showing your poems around Boston

Gave our family a sort of distinction,
The author being identified as
Phillis, African servant
Of John and Susannah Wheatley.
We were not vain,
God forbid vanity.
And pride.
So we could not be proud of you,
But we were....we were....
(Looks helplessly at Mary for a word.)

Mary: Pleased, Mamma, pleased
Is the word you want.
We were pleased.
The Wheatleys, all of us, were pleased.

Phillis: But I too am a Wheatley
Phillis Wheatley.
My name is Phillis Wheatley.

Susannah: The name we gave you, my dear.
You had no name.
We gave you one.
Phillis for the boat
That brought you from Africa
Wheatley, our name we shared.
But only shared, Phillis,
You never were a Wheatley.

Phillis: Then what was I?
                  Who was I?

Susannah: That we shall never know.
                  You were perhaps seven when I
                     bought you.

Nathaniel: Really, mother, could you not say 'found'.

Mary: Or 'saved'?

Susannah: Ah, yes, saved.
                  Yes, we saved you, Phillis
                  A sickly black child
                  Just shedding her baby teeth.
                  Yes, I often wondered
                  At that act of the benevolent Redeemer
                  That it was I, Susannah Wheatley,
                  Who saw you on that wharf
                  Wrapped in a bit of old carpet
                  And Christ's mercy swelled in my heart
                  And I chose you.
                  An act of Christian mercy.

Mary: Indeed, Mamma.
                  Although you did think the child
                  Could be taught simple household tasks
                  And would be a companion to you
                  When Nathaniel and I married
                  And left your household.

Susannah: No. My act was one of Christian charity.

Mary: Have it your own way, Mamma,
                Whatever, she proved quite useless
                In the household
                Dropping and breaking the vases she dusted.
                It was really to keep her occupied
                That you suggested Nathaniel and I
                Teach her to read.
                Your remark, as I recall, was,
                'To keep her out of mischief.
                Since we are saddled with her,
                Until she is strong enough
                And mature enough
                To be worth her purchase price.'

Nathaniel: As I recall, Mother, it was not much.
                Thin black children went for little.

Susannah: That is quite enough, Nathaniel.
                We bought her, whatever we paid.
                And she should be eternally grateful.

Phillis: Oh, I am.
                You gave me everything.
                I thanked you in the poems.

Nathaniel: Yes, you proved quite the little monkey
                In the poems. Could copy anything.
                Many a one remarked

That the poems were so English.
So male. So white.
They could have been written by Pope
Or Dryden.
When I took you to England
And had your poems published there,
I had to carry along a testimonial
Signed by 18 white New England males
Of high standing
Including Thomas Hutchinson
Royal Governor of Massachusetts
To prove that indeed you
Small black creature
That you still were at nineteen
Had really written them.

Mary: Yes, for a time you were
                Quite the wonder of the literary world.

Phillis: For a time.

Mary: *(quickly)*
                All changes, of course.
                There was the war.
                You married. We lost touch.

Phillis: *(quietly)*
                I died in poverty.
                My children died.

Mary: Yes. Hard years.
            Many children died in those years.
            We must not dwell on that.
            God's will be done.

Phillis: God's will.
            Was it God's will that I came to you?

Mary: Of course. You even wrote it in a poem.
            How it was God's will
            That we brought you from the
                darkness of Africa
            Into the light of New England
                Christianity.

Phillis: In the manner of Pope....

Mary: Or some other author of the time.

Phillis: In the manner of Pope...
            Then had I no manner of my own?

Nathaniel: What do you mean, your own?

Phillis: I mean...my voice,
            My own voice.
            Did I never speak to you in my own voice
            And not in the voice of Pope?

Mary: That is silly. How could you?

You had no words until I taught them
   to you.

Phillis: You taught me your words.

Mary: What else?

Phillis: Did you ever ask me mine?

Mary: Why should I?
                They would have been meaningless to me.

Phillis: But you never asked.

Mary: Heavens, no!
                And once you knew our language
                It seemed better never to question you
                About memories.
                God let you mercifully forget.
                Once you could speak
                You never spoke of memories.

Phillis: But I must have had them.

Nathaniel: You should be glad you forgot them,
                Were free to become the celebrity you became.

Phillis: Who did I become?

Susannah: What a silly! Phillis Wheatley, of course.

You know that.
You became Phillis Wheatley.

Phillis: But you say that is not my name
                    But only loaned.
                    And yet I have no other.
                    You took my name,
                    You took my past.
                    Who am I?

Nathaniel: *(laughing)*
                    You are Phillis Wheatley.

Mary: You are Phillis Wheatley.

Susannah: *(severely)*
                    You are Phillis Wheatley,
                    And you are lucky, Phillis Wheatley
                    That we have been willing
                    To spend all this time with you.
                    But we really must return
                    To the celestial kingdom
                    Where the amazing grace of our election
                    Has provided us with high seats.

(The three Puritans *stand stiffly and sing a Puritan hymn in unison as the lights fade. We hear Phillis' voice pleading with them not to leave her, but they keep on singing.)*

(When the lights come up again, the three have burlap taped again over the front of their costumes and the African masks before their faces. Phillis stares at them in disbelief. Then sits and weeps. In the background the masks begin to hum and from offstage comes a slow

*gradually increasing drum beat. All very quiet, but intense. Phillis lifts
her head. Music builds to a crescendo then stops abruptly.)*

Mask I: Black woman.

Phillis: *(sits quiet)*

Mask I: Black woman.

Phillis: Why do you call me that?

Mask I: Because I do not know your name
And wish to speak to you.
Tell me your name and I will use it.

Phillis: My name is...
I have no name.

Mask 2:   Surely you have a name.

Phillis: Perhaps once, long ago.
But I lost it.

Mask 3:   That is hard, to lose a name
Very hard.

Mask 2:   Have you tried to find it?

Phillis: No.

Mask 3:   No? That is strange.
           Surely you have looked for it.

Phillis: No.

Mask 2:   You just let it slip away?

Phillis: Yes, I just let it go.
           People, meaning to be kind, I suppose,
           Gave me another
           Or rather loaned me one.
           A borrowed name is all I have.
           It is a bitter thing
           To have no name.

Mask I: A bitter thing.
           But perhaps it can be found.
           You remember nothing?

Phillis: I have only one memory
           Of my mother kneeling facing the rising sun
           Praying silently to the dawn,
           Lifting a bowl of water above her head
           And then pouring it reverently on the earth.
           That memory clung and did not hurt so much
           Her face lifted to the dawn glistened with
              dark beauty.
           That I remember, but nothing more.
           Nothing.

Mask 2:   But now do you want to remember more?

Phillis: I don't know.
When I think of remembering, I am afraid.

Mask 3:   Of what?

Phillis: Of being slapped.

(She seems surprised at her own words.)

Mask 2:   Who would slap you for remembering?

Phillis: They...with the strange white faces.

Mask 1:   Why did they slap you?

Phillis: Because of my hand.
(cries out)
No! I don't want to remember

Mask 1:   *(insisting)* Why did they slap you?

Phillis: *(haltingly)* Because of my hand in the dish.

Mask 1:   Go on.

Phillis: *(This is difficult for her.)*
We are sitting at a great table
And they are there, all the white faces.
And I sit with them.

The chair is very tall
And they have placed a book on it
So that I can reach the table.
In the center of the table
Is the dish.
That I understand
The dish.
It is to dip the hand in.
And bring food to the mouth.
My mother would always say,
When a visitor came,
'Another hand to the dish.'

So I reach my hand to the dish.
I dip my hand in the dish
And bring food to my mouth.
The taste is strange
But I am very hungry.
I dip my hand again in the dish.

They do not notice.
Their heads are bowed
And one of them, a tall stern man,
Is intoning words I do not understand.
I dip my hand in the dish.
Then the words stop
And they all lift their heads.
My hand is in the dish. The faces
   look shocked.

Then my mistress who sits beside me
Reaches out her hand
And slaps my hand hard.
I draw back my hand.
She shouts at me, words I do not understand.
Then arms are dragging me from the table,
Carrying me up the stairs,
And shutting me in a room.
I huddle on the floor.
I hear the steps going away down the stairs
To the table where the food is
And I know it is wrong to remember
The hand in the dish.

I never sat at their table again
Indeed, looking back now,
I wonder I was there that first night.
Perhaps to show me off
Because, of course,
I belonged in the kitchen
With the other blacks.
Only there too I did not belong
I was black but I was a child.
They ignored me,
Fed me at a little table
By the stove.
But that first night,
Supperless, alone in the room,
I cried because I was hungry
And afraid.

Mask 1:   *(gently)*
            See, you have remembered a little.
            Perhaps you can remember more.

Phillis: I remember...
            No, I do not want to remember!
            When I remembered, I screamed in the night;
            Then they would scold me.
            I do not want to be scolded.

Mask 1:   We will not scold you.

Phillis: At night, at first memories did come.
            They stood around my bed
            Bad memories of arms snatching me,
            Stopping my mouth with a filthy rag,
            Tying my hands with rope that cut my wrists,
            Carrying me through the forest
            Until we came to the boat.
            Do not make me remember the boat.!

Mask I: There is no need for you to tell us
            About the boat.
            It is best to forget the boat.
            But perhaps now you can remember
            Other things not as hard as the boat.

Phillis: *(slowly)*
            I remember that at first I can only cry.
            But the white faces are cross when I cry.

So I sulk and hang my head.

They talk and I do not understand.
I remember only the words of my mother
And the sound of her voice
So low in the throat,
Not like the white voices
That are high and shrill
And seem to come from far away.

But the days go on
And the white voices seem closer
And louder
While the voice of my mother
Goes slipping off down the alley of memory
And when some of the white words
Carry meaning,
I raise my head
And look into their faces.
They are not unkind,
But they are not my mother.
I want a face to shine black in the sun,
But there is little sun where I am.
The air is cold
And the ground is white like the faces.

I wrap myself in my fears
Against the cold white faces.
The cold white ground.
I take a piece of charcoal from the hearth

And make a letter on the wall.
The white hand snatches away the charcoal
But it does not slap me.
For some reason, the voices are pleased,
As though they would caress me.

I pull away from the white hand.
For many days I pull away.
But my ears keep hearing the white voices
And as the days fill deeper with the
    white snow,
The white words pile up around me
And I understand what they say.

Then they are pleased.
I am quick to learn.
They smile and open books
And I read all the white words.
And the more I read the white words
The more the black words
Drift away into darkness.

And I write a poem.
It is not a child's poem
Though I am still a child.
It is not a black poem
Though I am black.
It is a poem like those in the book.
And I put on a white mask
For I am like the monkeys

And can copy what I see.

I do not see a child's poem
Or a black poem
Only a white poem
So I, black child,
Write them a white poem
And they are pleased and proud.

Wearing my mask
I give them my poem
And they carry it about
And show it
And carry me about and show me.

Only it is strange.
I must put on my black mask,
My child mask,
To read my white man's poem
And they call me a 'sooty prodigy'.
Then they carry me off to England
To show me as a 'sable muse'
And I am confused.

When I sit to write
I must wear my white mask.
When I stand to read
I must wear my black mask.
But neither is my face.
My face is back in Africa

Somewhere with my lost name.
(weeps)
Will I ever find my name?

Mask 1:   *(kneels beside her)*
Touch my face.

Phillis: *(shocked)*
What?

Mask 1:   Touch my face.

Phillis: *(drawing back)*
Oh, no.

Mask 1:   Do not be afraid.
If it hurts you to look on me,
Close your eyes and run your hand
    over my face.

(PHILLIS closes her eyes and puts out a timid hand. She runs it down the face of the mask, her head lowered. Then suddenly she raises her head.)

Phillis: It is the eland!
But he should be dancing.

Mask 1:   He will dance.
Be patient.

Phillis: Oh, when will he dance?
It is so beautiful when he dances

	With the fires leaping and drums throbbing
	And black bodies stamping.
	Oh let him dance!
Mask 1:	Be patient.
	First tell me what you see.
Phillis:	Sunlight...

With the fires leaping and drums throbbing
And black bodies stamping.
Oh let him dance!

Mask 1:   Be patient.
            First tell me what you see.

Phillis: Sunlight...
            The whole world flooded with sunlight
            And it is warm, so warm!
            My bare toes dig into the hot sand.
            We are standing in a great circle
            All the people of the village--
            The young boys, the women, the children.
            In the center are the men.
            They stand by the drums
            Their chests are bare
            But from their waists
            Hang loin cloths
            Red and gold and blue
            And colored thongs
            Stream from their wrists.
            Their faces are painted
            And bright bands circle their heads.

            And off to one side,waiting,
            Are the dancers.
            They are wearing their masks,
            The masks of the eland.
            They will dance

And bring many eland
Into our forests.
Oh, when will they dance?

Mask I: Soon.
They too are waiting.
And you are waiting.
What are you waiting for?

Phillis: I am waiting for my mother.
Always when the men dance
I stand by the dancing ring
And my mother holds my hand.
Where is my mother?

Mask I: She is coming.
Look, she is pushing through the crowd.
She is looking for her child.
Now she sees you.
She is calling to you.
Listen, can you hear what she is calling?

Phillis: She is calling my name!

Mask I: Now the eland can dance.

*(She opens her eyes, takes off her white mask, stands and lifts her
black face , ecstatic.)*

Phillis: He is already dancing!

Music up...lights dim...music fades...

Via Reggio Revisited

VIA REGGIO REVISITED was first presented at the Lenox
Library, Lenox, Massachusetts, on February 28, 1995 with the
following cast:

Claire Clairemont . . . . Jennifer Johanos

Lord Byron . . . . Glenn Barrett

August Leigh . . . . Elizabeth Petty

Mother . . . . Beth Bradley

Children . . . . Thais Bradley

                                          Malisa Bradley

Direction . . . . Frances Benn Hall

Via Reggio Revisited

Setting:	Beach at Via Reggio, Italy
Time:	The present. Night.
Characters:	Claire Clairmont
	Lord Byron
	Augusta Leigh
	Mother
	Children

(Darkness. Lights up, but not full. Beach. Night. Small dying fire up L. An indistinct woman in white is pacing the shore, staring out to sea. She gathers a few sticks. Picks up a discarded child's shovel and flings it down again. Takes her sticks up to the fire and adds them to it. Sits by fire, legs pulled up, arms hugging her knees.)

(Offstage, sound of splashing. She listens, stands. A man appears DL, shaking himself as though he has just risen from the sea. She stands, transfixed, then moves a step away from the firelight. Stage so dark that they cannot see each other's faces as they move toward each other.)

Claire: You came!

Byron: Augusta!

Claire: Out of the sea. Oh, I hoped you would come.

Byron: And I...I've searched everywhere
            But never really hoped to find you here.

Claire: Come to the fire where I can see you.

(Both have moved into spot of light. He starts to embrace her, then draws back angrily when he sees who it is.)

Byron: Hell! Claire!

Claire: And you called me....

Byron: Don't say it!
              I forbid you to speak her name.

Claire: You called me....

(He seizes her roughly and puts hand over her mouth. She struggles.)

Byron: Shut up, you bitch.
              Agreed? You do not say it?

(CLAIRE continues to struggle, then gives up and nods assent. He releases her. She stalks up to fire and plunks down moodily. He strolls up to her, in control now that he has silenced her.)

Byron: Very touching.
              Little Claire haunting Shelley's funeral pyre.
              What did you expect?
              That he would rise from the sea?
              You wouldn't like that, I can tell you.
              I saw him. You didn't.
              It wasn't pretty.
              We identified him from the book of poems
                 in his pocket.
              Why do you think we burned the body?
              There wasn't enough left to bury.

Claire:	Don't!
Byron:	Don't. Why not? What did you expect? A golden boy with lilies in his hair?
Claire:	I expected nothing. In life or in death. I've learned that, or thought I had. But you're right, I did come. This was one place I hadn't looked.
Byron:	Well, why ever you came, you're trespassing. Whatever you hoped to find, it isn't here. This is my stretch of beach, Nothing but sand and sea. At night even the tourists avoid it.
Claire:	Then why do you come?
Byron:	Because it's my beach. I earned it, by God!
Claire:	But that's not why you came. Why not admit it? This beach is a long shot for you too. Just for a minute, when you swam in And saw me here, you thought....
Byron:	Don't say it!
Claire:	Poor Byron. For all your worldly success

You are just as unhappy in eternity as I am.
Admit that at least.

Byron: I admit nothing.

Claire: And everything.
For a moment when you walked up the beach
I didn't recognize you.
Now I do.
How little you've changed.
Just as angry as you always were.
Only the limp is gone.
They did grant you that one prayer at least,
Two sound legs to walk through the
     pearly gates.
Pity you made that wish,
Perhaps one is all we get and you made two
And got the one that mattered less.

Byron: Well, whatever yours was
You don't seem to have gotten it either.

Claire: Evidently not.
But I couldn't know that for sure until I came.
But you wouldn't understand that.

Byron: But I do. It's pretty obvious
Your sitting here waiting for Shelley.
Oh, I may have been fooled, but not for long.
It was there from the start.

Shelley took you both on his honeymoon.
Odd decision, but he was an unusual man.
Eloped with two of Godwin's daughters
As the wags had it.
Loved you both, did he?

Claire: So that's your problem!
You think he was my lover.

Byron: Know it.
Oh, I admit you had me fooled at first.
My vanity accepted your coming up
  to London
To leap into my bed.
You threw yourself at me,
As other women had, I might add,
And I accepted what you offered.
You were very willing, and I was very able.
Despite my limp.

Claire: Your limp! Only you were so aware of it.

Byron: Strange, I quite often thought of little else.
And so I out-boxed them, out-swam them.
Byron climbs the Matterhorn,
Byron swims the Hellespont,
Byron declines to be the lame brat
His mother called him when she was angry
Which, by the way, she often was.

Claire: How sad.
             Because I only thought of you as handsome
                and virile.
             Never as lame.
             Why do you think I came to you in London?

Byron: Because your capacity for deceit
             Was greater than your fear of me.

Claire: Fear?

Byron: Yes, fear. You were shaking that night
                in London.
             I felt it as you lay in my arms.

Claire: Nonsense!

Byron: Not nonsense.
             You were playing a desperate game
             My wiley little Claire
             And the stakes were high.

Claire: I don't know what you're talking about.

Byron: But you do.
             Oh, I didn't know it at first
             But later it was transparent.
             You had to convince me
             And you were good, I'll give you that,
             And so for a while, too long, I believed.

And why not?
I had fathered other bastards.

Claire: But Allegra was your child. You know that.
             You claimed her, had her buried under
                your name.

Byron: Of course.
             Do you think I would let the world know
             How I had been duped?
             It was especially important that I claim her
             Once I knew it was Shelley's child
             You had foisted off on me.

             Oh, I had my suspicions
             Even before the brat was born.
             It was too pat.
             I knew you didn't love me,
             Neither in London when you threw yourself
                at me,
             Or later here in Italy
             When you persisted in prolonging the liaison,
             For Mary's benefit I suppose.
             You know how many nights
             You climbed through the grape arbors
             Up to castle Diodati
             And how many nights
             I declined to let you share my bed.
             Frankly, I found you *jejeune*, melancholy.
             You bored me.

And, admit it, you really did not need me
After an afternoon's dalliance with Shelley.

Claire: But that's untrue.
                 Shelley never slept with me.

Byron: I find that hard to believe.
                 Shelley slept with everyone.
                 It was a part of his artistic theory.
                 There was even a pattern.
                 Find a damsel in distress.
                 Rescue her,
                 Make love to her,
                 Write poems to her.
                 Then circle back to Mary's forgiving arms.
                 Shelley probably fathered as many bastards
                    as I did.
                 Mary even knew about some of them.
                 Offered to take them into her home.
                 As I said, she was forgiving.
                 But you she would never have forgiven.

Claire: No. You must believe me.
                 Allegra was yours. I swear it.

Byron: I daresay, Claire, that here in eternity
                 Swearing has little weight.
                 But it is unnecessary. I know.

Claire: And when did you know, as you insist
                 on believing?

Byron: Shelley gave it away; he importuned
                 too much.
               Kept begging me to give the child to you.
               Especially after Mary's and his children died.
               They had a pretty sorry track record
                 in that family.
               Children had a casual way of dying young.
               I had no intention of letting you get
                 hold of Allegra.
               And when he came to me in Venice,
               Begging to be allowed to see her in
                 her convent,
               He really overplayed his hand.
               That day I knew.

Claire: And yet you let him go to the convent
                 to see her.

Byron: To let him see what a beautiful child she
                 had become.
               The beautiful daughter he could never claim,
               Never have.
               He had betrayed me, and that I could
                 not forgive.
               I wanted to hurt him.
               And I did, by God, I did!
               You were not important enough to hurt.

Claire: But none of this is true.
               I could not have been pregnant
               When I came to you in London.
               I was a scared girl of 16.
               I had never slept with a man before.

Byron: That I do not believe.
               You were not inexperienced,
               And you lied to me from the start.
               As I pointed out,
               You three honeymooned together.
               Later, back in London,
               Mary found she was, as they coyly put it,
               'With child.'
               Shelley was delighted, of course,
               But when you turned out to be
               In the same condition,
               Something had to be done.
               Mary was jealous; she was, you know.
               You, the little step-sister,
               Were the prettier one,
               The gayer one,
               The one whose French was useful on
                 your travels.
               So something had to be done.
               And it was ingenious.
               Mary had her poet, and Shelley found
                 one for you.
               Sent you up to London to capture me.
               Then the three of you followed me to Italy

	To keep up the farce.
	And I, vain fool, slid into your lying net.
Claire:	Had any of this been true, which it wasn't,
	I must point out
	That you were quite easy to catch.
	You were so sure no one could resist you.
Byron:	So you admit it?
Claire:	Your outrageous scenario?
Byron:	No scenario, damn it, but the truth.
	That, I admit, for a time,
	I was too blind to see.
Claire:	*(pause)*
	How you hated him.
Byron:	Strangely, I did not.
	I was angry, I wanted to hurt him.
	And, by God, I did.
	But I rather admired him.
	He was a fine poet,
	And I felt his death such a ridiculous waste.
	After eight days the body was washed up.
	Trelawny and I burned it here on the beach.
	I will never forget that afternoon.
	The hot July sun, the pale burning sand.

The sky, cloudless and blue.
The sea lapping innocently in the sunlight,
And the pyre.

I sat by the fire, stirring the ashes.
Suddenly I could not stand it.
I ripped off my clothes
And dived naked into the sea,
Swam far out and flipped over on my back,
Just lay there floating, looking up at the sky
So blue, so cloudless, so vast,
So damned uncaring.

Then I swam back.
By then the fire was almost out.

Claire: As it is now.
We may as well go.
We have nothing to say to each other.
But there is one thing
I still don't understand.
Even if you believed this silly tale
Why did you keep Allegra from us?
We wanted her.
You found her a nuisance
After the novelty of showing her off
In your Venice palazzo wore off.
You hid her away in a cold convent.
She died there.
I loved her. Shelley loved her as his own,

Though she was not, I swear, she was not.
We begged you to give her to us.

You say you did not hate him.
Then, even if you believed your nonsense,
Why couldn't you let Shelley take her
From the convent?
Why did you persist in claiming a child
You neither loved nor wanted,
No matter whose you believed her to be?

Byron: You don't seem to have been listening!
Admit she was not mine
And hear the world laughing?
No indeed. I had plans for Allegra.
She was to be educated in the convent
And when she was 17,
I would have brought her out as my daughter.
Here in Italy there would have been
Any number of titled younger sons
Eager to marry her
Despite the shadow on her birth.

Unfortunately neither she nor I
Lived to see that happen.
But her tomb in England
Asserts my paternity
And so I won.

Claire: Was it, at the expense of the child,
           So necessary to win?

Byron: For me it always was, whatever the odds.

Claire: Even now, when it no longer matters?

Byron: But it does.
           Byron did not die in Greece.
           Byron lives.
           The poems remain in print
           The biographies keep rolling out.
           And Byron still controls what they say.
           Of course, I can't expect you to
               understand that.

Claire: Of course.
           I survive as a footnote at best.
           But strangely it does not matter.
           And do you know why?
           Because whatever you say
           I know what really happened
           And you are deluded still
           No matter what you have made
               the world believe.

           Do you want to know the whole truth?
           Why I came here tonight?
           What I hoped to find?

Byron: No, Claire, nothing about you ever
             mattered much.
           It certainly does not now.

Claire: You don't care that all my life
           I loved one person
           Not Shelley,
           And came here looking for him.

Byron: You sound like a bad Gothic novel.

Claire: That's all we were, weren't we,
           A bad Gothic novel?
           But if we were
           Is it still necessary to be so cruel now?

Byron: Life hurt us.
           Eternity hurts us.
           We try to hurt back.
           It's simple.

Claire: Ah, the hurt, it keeps you so bitter.
           At least I seem to have moved beyond
             bitterness.
           I came, not really hoping
           And that was at least a blessing.
           I shall not come again.

Byron: Nor shall I.

Claire: Then it was not as you said.
            This was a first time for you too
            Your long shot--and you failed too.

Byron: I never fail, and I had no long shot.
            I told you, bitch, this is my beach.
            I earned it.

Claire: No. Tonight, for some reason,
            Impossible as you felt it to be
            You were drawn here,
            Came hoping to find her
            Because it was one place you hadn't looked.

Byron: Come off it!
            I have no idea what you are talking about.
            Nor interest in knowing.

Claire: But you do.
            When I walked out of the firelight,
            Moved toward you in the darkness,
            You mistook me. You called me....

Byron: I warned you.....

Claire: *(Goes steadily on.)*
            Afraid I might say her name?
            Come, we have talked of other things.

            I have tried to be candid and honest,

Though you persist in not believing me.
Can we not talk of her?

Byron: I have nothing to say.

Claire: But you do.

Come, talk to me of the agony

Of loving your sister.

(BYRON *is suddenly overcome with violent chills. He shudders, sits
huddled, hugging his knees and shaking.* CLAIRE *kneels behind him,
pulls off her shawl and wraps it around his shoulders, cradles him and
during the scene mothers him.*)

Claire: What is it? What is it?
There. You'll be all right.
You're chilled, that's all.
You came out of the water
Into the night air.
It's just a chill.

Byron: I'm so cold.
So cold up here.
So cold on these Alps.
I told Shelley we should turn back,
But he would not listen, and I could
  not insist.
He would think I was favoring my leg
And I chose never to favor my leg.

Claire: There...there. Your leg is all right.

You're here with me on the beach.
You just have a chill.

(BYRON *pulls free from her, rises, shaking but pacing.*)

Byron: So we didn't turn back, but kept on climbing
And the snow started coming down
    faster and faster.

(He tramps through imaginary snow.)

But we kept on climbing
Couldn't see where we were going,
But kept on going
And night came
But the moon was bright on the snow
And we climbed and climbed, on and on
And then suddenly it was dawn
And the snow had stopped
And we were on the top of a frozen world
Just two lone men
On the very top of a world of glass
And the sun on the ice sparkled like diamonds.

I knew a moment of such exhilaration
I turned to Shelley and threw my arms
    about him.
I hugged him close, called him my brother,
The brother I never had.
He stood dumb in my embrace,
Then pulled from me, walked away from me,

His boots making deep cuts
In the virgin snow.
Just walked away to stop at the edge
  of the cliff,
Stand there, his back to me
Looking down over the valley far below.
Not speaking.

I said again, my brother
And he said, not looking at me
No man has a brother
We climb alone
And at the top there is nothing but
  the descent
Swifter than the climb, but ending always
In the abyss.
And yet stupidly we climb.

I stood frozen, horrified,
That he, bright angel,
Saw only the abyss that haunted me.
That for all his messages of hope
He too was hopeless.

Hopeless.
Dante was wrong.
Abandon all hope
Was not written above hell
But above earth
And hell is not hot

>   But cold...cold...cold.
>   I'm so cold.

Claire: Alba, Alba, come. The fire is brighter.
            Sit here by me. Let me warm you.

(BYRON is led like a child to the fire.)

Byron: Don't scold me for being a lame brat
            And wandering off into the snow.
            Don't scold me, Mother.

Claire: I'm not your mother.
            It's Claire.
            You're here with me.
            You were in the water.
            You got chilled.
            It's all right.

(BYRON stops shivering, looks around, is back to himself, bitter.)

Byron: Chilled. Cosmic irony. Chilled in hell.
            But it's not even hell, is it?
            It's just this nothingness,
            This eternal nowhere.
            Oh God, what irony, what cosmic irony.
            I hated my life.
            I longed for my death.
            In life there was only one happiness
            And that denied me
            Augusta, my sister,

The only one in the world I ever
  loved, wanted.
All the arms of all the women of the world
Could not take away the pain
Of wanting to lie in her arms.
All the arms of the young Greek boys
I bought to hug me were lifeless
Because they were not her arms.
Only Augusta ever mattered
And that was my consolation
As I lay in my tent dying,
Knowing I was dying.
My consolation was the thought
That in hell we would be forever damned
Like Paolo and Francesca
Sinners, doomed
In each other's arms.
Locked in the embrace of the damned
Brother and sister in each other's arms.

We deserved hell more than they.
Surely incest was a greater sin than
  mere adultery
Shelley was right, no man has a brother
Only a sister...a lost sister.

Claire: Poor Alba.

Byron: *(springing up)*
                 Don't pity me! I want no pity.

You always were a witch
And now you think you have tricked
  me again.
I deny speaking to you.
I deny anything you may think I have said.
I have never been here.
It is a mirage, a trick of moonlight.
I'm leaving and I advise you to leave too.
Your golden boy will never rise from the sea.

(He starts off, kicks something; picks up toy shovel.)

Byron:

A toy shovel.
Here.

(tosses it to her)

Should you meet up with that dear pledge
We've been arguing about,
Tell her it's a present from Papa.

(CLAIRE rushes at him, hits him. He parries blows, laughing.)

Claire:

Damn you! Damn you!

Byron:

Naughty, naughty.
You forget eternity is wide.
May our paths never cross again.

(He rushes off to dive into sea.)

Claire:

You bastard, oh, you egocentric bastard.
It's not all about you.
Tonight it was about me.
Don't you understand? I came for you.

And you, you couldn't even see me
Whining about Augusta
Forbidding me to speak her name.
I'll speak it. I'll shout it.
AUGUSTA....AUGUSTA....AUGUSTA...

What a fool I was
To think eternity might have softened him.
He's just as arrogant and cruel
As he always was.
I LOVE YOU. YOU BASTARD,
In spite of everything
And I'll shout it if I want to.
AUGUSTA...AUGUSTA...AUGUSTA...

(AUGUSTA *enters.)*

Augusta: Did you call me? I was...elsewhere
                And seemed to hear my name.

Claire: Taken in wrath, I assure you.
                But you're welcome to stay.
                I'm just leaving.

Augusta: A lovely beach, sand and moonlight
                And a fire. Were you expecting someone else?

Claire: I can't see that is any of your business.

Augusta: Forgive me.

Claire: He came. He's gone.
             I'm not sure he even saw me.

Augusta: But you spoke to him.

Claire: I spoke at him. Not the same thing.
             He was looking for someone else.

Augusta: Ah.

Claire: You, of course.

Augusta: How sad.
             Because I can't grieve that I missed him.

Claire: Well, you came.

Augusta: Because I was called.

Claire: But you must have had some idea
             Of what it might concern.
             You didn't have to come.
             Why are you here?

Augusta: Touchez!
             I admit I think of him sometimes,
             Pity him really.
             He was just a frightened little boy
             Bragging about how big and bad and
                 wicked he was.

<table>
<tr><td></td><td>Orgies and incest
And see me swim the Hellespont!
That at least he did do.</td></tr>
<tr><td>Claire:</td><td>But the rest?</td></tr>
<tr><td>Augusta:</td><td>Fantasy mostly.
I know for a fact the incest was.
It didn't happen.
Perhaps for his sake it should have.
Perhaps if I had slept with him just once
He could have forgotten about it.
But at the time I thought
That it was enough for him
That the world believed it true.</td></tr>
<tr><td>Claire:</td><td>But you did love each other.</td></tr>
<tr><td>Augusta:</td><td>My dear, I was his sister, years older than he.
I had children of my own.
I loved him as one loves a lonely moody child.</td></tr>
<tr><td>Claire:</td><td>And the gossip didn't bother you?</td></tr>
<tr><td>Augusta:</td><td>Oh, I too was a rebel in my own way.
Perhaps I should have cared about the gossip.
Instead, I'm afraid it amused me
That London was so monstrously shocked
By a rumor so patently untrue.</td></tr>
</table>

Claire: But he did make the world believe it.

Augusta: He made the world believe many things.
               All compensating, of course,
               For that wretched club foot.

Claire: He doesn't have it anymore.

Augusta: No? Strange that he was granted that wish
               And it's not enough, of course.

Claire: No, he wants to suffer
               To burn with you in hell
               Like Paolo and Francesca.

Augusta: The Dante syndrome.
               How so many people could believe
               That a fourteenth - century Italian poet
               Could map the hereafter
               And let us know what to expect.
               I gather you've found conditions different
               From your expectations?

Claire: Oh, I expected nothing really.
               I outlived my expectations.

Augusta: And yet you came here tonight, why?

Claire: Because it's here, this beach
               A hard reality that goes on.

Because everyday living people still walk it
Mostly unaware of what happened here once.
It seemed to me that that...the hard reality
Of sand and sea might pull a ghost
To be here too.

Augusta: Shelley?

Claire: No, not Shelley.
                Oh, everyone has it wrong about
                    me and Shelley.
                No matter what Mary and the
                    world believed.
                He was my friend, my only friend, probably.
                But lover, no.
                For all the reputation I seem to have acquired,
                I was naively monogamous
                I loved only once.

Augusta: My brother.

Claire: Yes. And he never loved me. Never.
                Hated me because I tricked him
                Into letting me into his bed.
                So he took away my child, our child.
                I soon knew I could not have Byron
                But I wanted his son.
                Irony there. I had a daughter.
                Perhaps had she been a son
                He might have loved me.

But I had a daughter.
Oh, there was a bit of him in her,
The dark curls, the lonely defiance.
I should have seen that,
Should have settled for Allegra.

Augusta: But why did you give her to him?
Surely the child meant something to you.

Claire: Something. But not enough.
I thought he would grow to love her
And through her, love her mother.
I was wrong.
And once I realized it,
Gave up hoping and tried to get her back,
It was too late.
And I did it all wrong.
I let Shelley try to help me.

Augusta: What could have been wrong in that?

Claire: Because, although we didn't know it then,
It gave him the idea
That the child was Shelley's.
He told me so tonight.
Even seemed to take a masochistic pleasure
In insisting in believing it.

Augusta: So the mistake
Was giving her to him in the first place.

Claire: I was stupid.
                   I loved him more than I loved her.
                   I was 18,
                   Living on the fringes of their exciting world.

                   Shelley wrote *Adonais*
                   Byron wrote *Don Juan*
                   Mary wrote *Frankenstein*
                   And Claire...
                   Claire had neat handwriting
                   And for a time was useful
                   Copying manuscripts for Byron.
                   And irony of ironies
                   I felt it a great honor.
                   I used to stay up far into the night
                   Recopying a page that bore the slightest blot
                   And in the morning
                   Climb up through the grape arbors
                   To Castle Diodati
                   To place the pages in his hand.
                   Although he often grabbed them rudely
                   And flung them onto his desk
                   Without looking at them.

                   But at least he let me come
                   And I was a part of his world.
                   But once I told him there would be a child,
                   He rarely slept with me.
                   I was allowed to continue the copying
                   Because it was useful.

Augusta: But later....

Claire: Years brought a bit of maturity, I suppose.
                I found I missed her.
                I had not thought to miss her, but I did.
                As I played with Mary's child
                I found myself thinking of my own
                And wanting her back.
                And then when Shelley saw her in the convent
                And brought me back a lock of her hair,
                I treasured it.
                But even then I was still a fool.
                I treasured that lock of hair
                Because it was raven black, like his.

                You see, that was the mistake,
                That I always loved him more.
                Fool that I was
                I really thought that some day
                He would tire of his concubines
                And slave boys
                And realize it was me he loved.
                And after Allegra died--
                She was only five--
                After she died, that was all I had to hope for

                That even though there was no child
                To pull us together
                He would come to me.

Then he died too
And I lived on--too long
And because life was empty
I began counting on eternity.
Well, tonight, after all the years
He did come.
But it was not for me he was looking.

Augusta: My dear, perhaps it is different than
                   you think.
               You say you came here looking
                   for someone.
               Could it be you were drawn here
               By someone looking for you?

Claire: *(bitterly)*
               No one in eternity is looking for me.
               And you're wrong
               I know exactly why I came
               Hoping against hope
               To find him.
               And he came. But not for me.

               Suddenly tonight I wanted to hate him
               To hurt him.
               I screamed at him and struck him
               But he only held my wrists and laughed
               And dived back into the sea.

Augusta: Forget him. Forgive him if you can.

Even eternity is not perfect.
Try to forget the man
Who was often weak and cruel
And remember the poet
Who when his mask was down
Let us see he was tortured too.

'The race of life becomes a hopeless flight
To those that walk in darkness; on the sea
The boldest steer but where their ports invite
But there are wanderer's o'er eternity
Whose bark drives on and on, and anchored
   ne'er shall be.'

Claire: Bravo, Augusta,
Quoting *Child Harold*.
But I'm afraid poetry isn't enough for me.

Augusta: And I have nothing else to offer you.
Even here, we are just small pieces
In a vast design
We don't understand.
Perhaps it is still whirling
To a completion
We cannot see.

I have no answers
I wish I had.
I might as well have stayed...elsewhere.

Claire: Then why don't you hie elsewhere.
             I'm sure you have hosts of people waiting
                for you.

Augusta: How bitter you are.
             It is true, I have found eternity
                quite peaceful.
             Perhaps you will too when you stop
                fighting it.

Claire: Spare me your pieties.

Augusta: Forgive me. They were well meant.

(She attempts to embrace CLAIRE, *who lashes out and strikes at her.)*

Claire: How dare you touch me!
             How dare you pity me!
             I don't need your pity.
             Just go, for God's sake
             And leave me in peace!

Augusta: I could wish it were in peace.
             Perhaps that will come in time.

*(*AUGUSTA *exits.* CLAIRE *paces beach, picks up the toy shovel and flings it down again.* CHILD *appears.)*

Claire: Allegra, you came!

Child: *(draws back)*
             I'm not who you said.

I'm Molly.
I came for my shovel.

Claire: *(Hurt, but adjusting; self-angry at own credulity)*
Molly. What a nice name.
For a monment
I thought you were another little girl
That I knew a long time ago.

Child: That's silly.
If you knew her a long time ago
She would be bigger.

Claire: Of course she would.

Child: I'm not supposed to talk to strangers.
I just want my shovel.

Claire: I found your shovel. It's over here.

(CLAIRE *moves to spot where shovel lies, kneels to pick it up.* MOTHER *of child enters.)*

Mother: Molly, how dare you sneak out of the cottage!
We were worried sick until I thought to
    look here.

Child: I came for my shovel.
The nice lady found it.

Mother: Don't add lying to the rest of it.

> There is no nice lady and you know it.
> Lady indeed!
> I find you alone on the beach
> And you start talking about nice ladies.

Child: But I'm not lying. See, there she is.

Mother: There certainly is no lady.
              But I do see your shovel lying over there.
              Now run and pick it up.

(CHILD *crosses. CLAIRE kneels by shovel, not touching it. When child reaches to pick it up, CLAIRE touches the child gently on the cheek. CHILD submits, then grabs shovel and runs to her mother who drags her off, child looking back at CLAIRE over her shoulder.)*

(CLAIRE *kneels a moment, then crosses up to fire and picks up her shawl. She stares out across water.)*

Claire: 'And there are wanderer's o'er eternity
              That anchored ne'er shall be.'

(*She exits.)*

(Stage is empty; music as in beginning. Then a child, a different one, smaller, around five, dark haired, wearing an old-fashioned white-ruffled night dress--or white dress--appears upstage. She walks down center as though looking for someone. She looks. There is no one. Music and lights fade.)

Blackout.

(Note: In the original production, Byron's only "Claire" poem, sung from offstage to guitar accompaniment, was used to open and close the play.)

There be none of Beauty's daughters
With a magic like thee
And the music on the waters
Is thy sweet voice to me.

Lucia

Lucia

Characters: Lucia Joyce, age 33
Giorgio Joyce, age 35
Doctor
Narrator
Teacher
2 extras.

(The staging is very simple, played on a bare stage.

UR at back is a raised platform, about four feet high, on which Narrator sits behind desk. He is impersonal, above and outside the action. He makes brief announcements and flips Brechtian cards on which words are large enough for audience to read.

*UL, but a bit farther downstage is a lower platform needed to raise teacher figure above height of child-*LUCIA.

Lucia's cot DR in pool of light; second pool of light DL. General lighting for dance scenes.)

*(*LUCIA *wears a formless white nightgown, child-like and innocent; she is thin and frail; her long hair often falls over her face and must be pushed wildly aside. Her moods and speeches shift violently from hallicinating to lucid. She must be able to dance.)*

(Blackout. Light comes up on spot DL).

Doctor: I doubt if she will recognize you. At times we have had to restrain her. It is almost as though she senses what has happened. Impossible, of course.

Giorgio: Perhaps not. My father felt her to be clairvoyant. She may know.

Doctor:	I doubt it. The wild stabs of the insane at times hit near the mark, but it is, in my opinion, pure chance. However, if your news upsets her further, as I fear it will, attendants will be nearby. And I beg you, be brief. I doubt if you will reach her at all and see no reason to prolong the visit.
Giorgio:	Leave that to me. I have known her a long time.
Doctor:	I doubt if anyone has ever known Lucia, but do your best. I don't envy you the job. Though if it sends her into a tail spin, I'll be dealing with it long after you are gone.

*(He exits L. G*IORGIO *crosses stage to DR; lights come up on* L*UCIA* *sitting very still and straight on edge of small white-covered cot.)*

Giorgio:	*(tentatively)* Lucia...Lucia....
Lucia:	Why do you call me Lucia? I am Iphigenia. Can't you see? Because of me the ship could sail. Without me. No Trojan war. And no ULYSSES. Do you hear me? No ULYSSES!!!!!

Giorgio: Lucia, there is something I must tell you.

Lucia: There is nothing you can tell me.
                I understand it all.
                Oh, he was clever.
                He disguised me
                So they think I am Milly Bloom
                Or Iseult Earwicker
                And babble of incest.
                They can only see that side of love.
                Incest, ha!
                Had it been even that
                It might have been enough
                Because I needed love
                Any kind of love
                Love
                Do you understand me? LOVE!!!!!

Giorgio: Lucia, your father....

Lucia: *(draws herself up)*
                My father is a famous author.
                Did you know that?
                He has written the most famous book in
                  the world.
                It is called *Ulysses*.

Giorgio: Your father....

Lucia: My father was not married to my mother.

Did you know that?
I was a bastard.
When my mother was angry, she called
  me a bastard.
She was right.
I hated my mother.
But she was right.
I was a bastard.
And I was ugly.
My eyes were crossed.
I hated my eyes.
I hated myself.
I was stupid.
Do you hear me? Stupid.

Giorgio: You were not stupid.
You had many talents.
Think of the alphabets you drew.

Lucia: Alphabets.
That is funny. Very funny.
Me and alphabets.
I lived in a whirl of alphabets.

(She moves out to center stage and spins like a child. A tall imposing female teacher appears on platform L.)

(In this aphabetical-school series, the TEACHE*r will always begin her questioning of the child in the language of the city that is indicated on the placard. She and Lucia will then proceed to play the scene in English with the hope that the audience will understand what language is really being employed. If handled with care, this should be clear to the audience ala Friel in his play,* Translations.*)*

Narrator: *(Displays placard:TRIESTE.)*

Teacher: *(in Italian)*
                 Attenzione!

Lucia: *(Stops whirling and stands before teacher looking
                 small.)*

Teacher: *(in Italian)*
                 Come si chiama?

Lucia: My name is Lucia Joyce.

Teacher: Where were you born?

Lucia: Here in Trieste.

Narrator: *(matter of factly)*
                 In the pauper's ward. Her father was
                 hospitalized elsewhere and was not present.

Teacher: How old are you?

Lucia: I was five in July.
                 But I can spell my name. L U C I A.

Teacher: That is good. Here you will learn more and
                 be happy.

(LUCIA *whirls happily away singing a child's song in Italian.*)
(*Her gay mood is halted by clapping of teacher on platform.*)

Narrator: (*Displays placard: ZURICH.*)

Teacher: (*in German*)
                 Wie heisst du?

Lucia: (*in Italian*)
                 Mi chiama Lucia Joyce.

Teacher: Speak German!

Lucia: I don't know German.
                 I can only speak Italian.

Teacher: Here we speak German.
                 You must be put back in the baby class.
                 How old are you?
                 I said HOW OLD ARE YOU?

Lucia: (*Intuits the question, but has no answer. She holds up
                 fingers on both hands. The audience should be able to
                 see she is only eight.*)

(*Offstage we hear children singing a German folk song..*LUCIA *stands
dumbly, unable to join in.*)

Narrator: (*Displays placard: TRIESTE*)

Teacher: (*in Italian*)
                 Come si chiama?

Lucia: *(in German)*
              Ich heisse Lucia Joyce.

Teacher: Speak Italian please.
              You are in Trieste, not Zurich.
              Here we do not speak German.
              How old are you?

Lucia: *(in German)*
              Zwölf.

Teacher: Speak Italian.
              (in Italian)
              Dolice.

Lucia: *(in Italian)*
              Dolice.

(LUCIA stands there...counts to 11 rather quickly and defiantly in German, but when she reaches the number 12 screams it out in Italian several times.)

(TEACHER, now being French teacher, rings bell to attract her attention.)

Narrator: *(Displays placard: PARIS.)*

Teacher: *(in French)*
              Comment vous appellez-vous?

Lucia: Je m'appelle Lucia Joyce, and I am thirteen
              years old.

Teacher: French please. At this lycee we speak only
             French. I can see you are not fit to enroll. I
             shall recommend that you not be admitted
             until you learn the languge!

             (LUCIA moves dejectedly back and sits on bed.)

Lucia: In school I was always stupid.
             But stupid people can draw.
             That was why he suggested the alphabets
             When I cried and cried about dancing.
             Did you know I danced?
             Dancing. It is wonderful.
             You do not need words and alphabets
               for dancing.
             But it is not easy, dancing.
             You must work and work
             And study with the right people.
             I worked and worked.
             I studied with all the right people.
             And I loved to dance.

*(She rises and strips off her nightgown, wears a green-blue leotard. She
moves to center stage and begins her exercises.)*

*(NARRATOR on platform reveals cards that name the companies with
whom she studied. Nationalities of companies indicated by names being
superimposed on card colored like country's flag. These include:
Cours Jaques Dalcroze (Swiss), Cours Jean Borlin (Swedish), Cours
Madika (Hungarian), Raymond Duncan (American), Egrova (Russian),
Louis Hutton and Helene Vanel (rhythm and color), and Margaret Morris
(modern).)*

(In this sequence her movements become more complex and raced as the schools go by faster and faster...accompanied by offstage music. This sequence must be worked out with NARRATOR, LUCIA and music. It must be carefully coordinated so audience will understand the intensity of her struggle and again the multiple breaks in the pattern...the shifting from one to another in a frantic effort to achieve, be accepted....)

(LUCIA stops spinning...music stops...she moves languidly down R to GIORGIO....)

Lucia: And finally I danced in concerts.
And for my last concert, I designed my
   own dress.
It was a beautiful dress...
Silver, like a fish

(She leaves downstage area and moves up R to platform where NARRATOR calmly hands her the fish dress. It is silver and shimmery and when she puts it on over her greenish leotard she looks fish-like.)

Lucia: I put on the dress.
And the music started.
(it does)
And I slid through the air.
Oh, Giorgio, I was a fish
Sliding through the river.
I danced for my father.
So he would be proud
And pleased.

(Dance...a real dance...well done.....she is exultant.)

Lucia: And when I finished
The audience clapped and clapped.
I stood there behind the curtain

And cried because I was so happy.
The audience was clapping and clapping
And I dried my eyes and went out.
People rushed up, praising me
But I tried to push through them
Looking for him.
Then I saw him over in a corner,
Surrounded by journalists.
I went to him
And he put his arm around me,
But he went on talking
Telling them about his books
And flash bulbs snapped.

Next morning there was a picture of us
On the front page of the morning paper
And do you know what the caption said:

Narrator: *(coldly)*
                 James Joyce, world famous author of *Ulysses*
                 with one of the dancers at a recital at the
                 Bal Bullier.

Lucia: One of the dancers.....
                 And I knew then
                 That I was ......
                 Only one of the dancers.

*(She removes her fish dress, lets it fall to floor and puts on nightgown
slowly.)*

And I took my fish dress and hid it under
   my bed
And I never danced again.
He agreed.
He said, Ah yes, the dance is too physical
   for you.
Why don't you draw alphabets?
So I drew alphabets
That were published because I was
   his daughter
Not because I could draw alphabets.
I hated the alphabets!
I hated the schools!
I hated my mother!
I hated Samuel Becket who came to see my
   father, not me!
I hated my life!
I was nobody.

But now I know who I am.
Now I am happy.
Do you know who I am?
Come closer
I will whisper it to you.
I am Iphigenia.

Giorgio: Lucia, listen to me, please.
                  You must try to understand.
                  He is dead. Papli is dead.

Lucia: *(Stares at him, then laughs.)*
                Dead? What is he doing under the
                    ground, that idiot?
                When will he decide to come out?
                He is watching us all the time!

                (Laughs hysterically.)

Giorgio: Oh, Lucia....

Lucia: Lucia?
                I am not Lucia.
                I am Iphigenia.
                Agamemnon loved Iphigenia.
                He only sacrificed her to the Gods
                Because the Gods made him.
                Don't you understand that?
                THE GODS MADE HIM DO IT!

                (Hysterically she beats at Giorgio.)

                THE GODS MADE HIM!
                BUT HE LOVED HER.
                HE LOVED HER!!!!!!

                *(Hysterical screaming...attendants rush in with strait jacket and force
                her into it as lights go down on her area. We hear her still screaming
                and screaming and laughing and laughing in the darkness. Then lights
                come up on narrator who impersonally says.)*

Narrator: Lucia Joyce never left the sanitarium and died
                there on December 12, 1982, the eve of St.
                Lucia's Day, at age 75, 41 years after the
                death of her famous father.

The Book of Herself

THE BOOK OF HERSELF was first presented at the Lenox Library, Lenox, Massachusetts, on January 20, 1996, with the following cast:

Lady Gregory . . . . Jennifer Johanos
Grania . . . . Kathy Jo Barrett
Dancers . . . . D J McDonald
                                               Laurie Bemis
Musicians . . . . Glenn Barrett
                                                Elizabeth Petty
Young Boy . . . . Michael Wartella
Direction . . . . Frances Benn Hall

The Book of Herself

Setting: On Ben Bulben
                    A mountain near Silgo

Time: The present. Evening

Characters: Lady Gregory
                    Grania
                    Dancers
                    Musicians
                    Young Boy

(Two MUSICIANS toil into view after a long climb up Ben Bulben. They sit, panting.)

Second: Why have you dragged us here
                    To the bare top of Ben Bulben?
                    There is nothing here
                    But windswept rock
                    And circling daws.

First: Because the churchyard was bare
                    And Drumcliff brought us nothing.
                    We could have played
                    Til the night was gone
                    And conjured no spirits.
                    Even the golden swans
                    On the church doors
                    Seemed to sneer at our hoping
                    To find matter for song

In that spot.
Drumcliff has been mined.

Second: But to climb Ben Bulben....

First: They did.

Second: Who would you be talking of now?

First: Those who came before us
Who peopled the old legends.
Their spirits could walk
Of an evening on these bleak rocks.
Come, let us sit,
Gaze across the valley.
There's Maive's tomb crowning
   Knocknera.
The heroes of the Red Branch,
Finn and his bands,
They all roved here.
Take up your flute.
Its notes could pull a spirit
Out of time
Or call one back
Like Oisin from Tir nan og.

(They sit to stage left and begin to play.)

First: Listen. I heard a pebble fall
And the rush of wind
Like a vanished host.

> Someone is coming
> Summoned by our plaining airs.

(He stands, moves out and looks down mountain.)

First: But no, this is no fairy host
                  Or warrier band.
                  Only a woman in widow's black
                  A stout stick in her hand.
                  I had expected worthier prey.

*(*Lady Augusta Gregory*, in widow's weeds, enters R, panting.)*

Lady Gregory: Where am I now
                  And the light fading in the west?
                  Atop a mountain, surely
                  And it a steep one
                  And I breathless.

                  As a girl I often climbed
                  Connemara's rocky bens
                  And hid in heather
                  My lonely grief
                  At not being comly
                  As my sisters were.

                  But later there was no need to climb.
                  I paced the Abbey greenroom
                  With a queen's tread
                  Or welcomed famous guests to Coole.
                  So why am I in this windswept place?

To be brought back to Coole Park
I could understand.
Though the house is gone
The autograph tree,
The ilex lane,
Still stand.
I could be glad to walk
The seven woods again,
Or sit beneath the catalpa

Counting the paired swans
And they still gliding there.

Why Ben Bulben?
For I see now it is Ben Bulben,
The churchyard lying below
And off to the West, the sea.
Why Ben Bulben?
Yeats' Sligo was never mine.
There must be some mistake

(GRANIA *enters L; wears Celtic dress of third-century.*)

Grania: No mistake.
               You came for me....

Lady Gregory: Should I know you?

Grania: As well as your own heart.
               It was you conjured me

And gave me words, brave words, to speak.
Listen.

> *What way could I live beside him?*
> *What name might I be calling out in*
>   *my sleep?*
> *It would be a terrible thing,*
> *A wedded woman,*
> *To call out another man's name*
> *In her sleep.*

Brave words
But never spoken
For you stopped my mouth.

Lady Gregory: Ah then, I do know you.
                  Grania, the only child I denied.

Grania: Grania, who spoke your heart's words truly.

Lady Gregory: Too truly to let them be spoken
                  On the Abbey stage.
                  Your story cut too close
                  The bone of mine.

Grania: So you denied me life.

Lady Gregory: I felt it better so.

Grania: For you. But what of me?

And I yearning to tell my story,
More poignant than that of Deirdre.

Lady Gregory: Yours was a different story, Grania.
You did not follow your love into death
As Deirdre did.
You returned to your old husband.

Grania: As you did.
You lived ten years more
With that old man who coughed and wheezed
In the marriage bed.

Lady Gregory: And you?
Did Finn leave you alone
After Diarmuid's death
When in your haughty pride
You foreswore Diarmuid
And your love?
Did Finn leave you alone?

Grania: The answer to that you know
Though leaving it out of your play.
Of course he did not.
I lying beneath him, gritting my teeth,
And accepting his sweaty embraces.
You understand that well enough.
Though in your luck,
Your man was old and died
And you could sleep alone

In the great bed at Coole.

Lady Gregory: You go too far!
How dare you speak such insolence!
Sir William was a kind and honorable man.
I mourned his passing all my life.

Grania: It was widow's weeds you wore, surely,
But in mourning was it,
Or in penance?

Lady Gregory: How dare you...

Grania: I dare much
Having caught you out at last
And it is before we leave
This spot
That I shall be having my say.
I ask you again
Was it in penance
That you wore those dreary weeds,
In penance that you sent away
To school, Robert,
The constant reminder
Of those unwelcome gropings?

Lady Gregory: You dare far too much.
I doted on Robert.

Grania: Tried to. Perhaps you did

And grieved his death
For many years.
But admit.
Robert was a disappointment.

Lady Gregory: That is unfair.
Robert did much--
Designed beautiful sets
For the Abbey,
Painted pictures
That hang in the National Gallery,
Yeats called him a second Sidney
'Soldier, scholar, horseman.'

Grania: Yeats wrote that poem
Reluctantly
Importuned by you.
Read it carefully.
It takes him fifty lines
To get to his subject.

Lady Gregory: Robert died young
Before there was time
For him to reach his worth.

Grania: Not that young.
He was middle-aged.
And though he painted,
Rode to hounds,
Married and fathered children,

He never found himself.

Yeats saw that,
Robert's unfulfilled life,
It is all there in his real poem about Robert
'An Irish Airman Foresees His Death'
You hated that poem, tried to suppress it
Because in it your son
Welcomes his death
As an escape from you and Coole.
No, he was a disappointment.
Not the son who might have been sired
By the other...the poet....

Lady Gregory: I forbid you to speak his name.

Grania: Whose name do you forbid me to speak?
                  Yeats?
                  Oh that game never took me in.

Lady Gregory: I do not have to listen to your insolence.

Grania: But you do.
                  We are bound here, you and I.
                  Take a step.
                  See, you cannot.
                  Not until we have this out,
                  Until you tell me
                  What I need to make you say,
                  Why, having created me

> You stopped my mouth,
> Decreed Grania could never
> Walk the Abbey stage
> While you yet lived.
>
> Come, the sooner you unburden
> The sooner this meeting may end.

Lady Gregory: Very well, then sit.
For the story may be long
In the telling
And dawn may break
Before it is ended.

(They sit.)

Lady Gregory: It may be hard for you to
understand, Grania,
For you were beautiful
And in the legends
Always young and fleet of foot.
When Finn stood on the hill,
Prize for the girl
Who could first ascend it,
You, daughter of a king,
Were the first to reach him.
That has always puzzled me a little.
Why did you vie to be bride
Of that old man?

Grania: Because I was lonely and bored at Tara

Because I had not then seen
  Diarmuid.

Lady Gregory: Ah yes, now I understand.
I too was lonely and bored,
Eleventh child in a lusty family of 16.
And small and slight and overlooked.
Until at 28
I felt no one could love me
And vied to capture any man
Even one older than my father.
Married him, bore a child,
And then, two years later,
Met the most beautiful man
I ever saw.

Grania: More beautiful than Yeats?

Lady Gregory: Oh, Willie was a boy,
Handsome and troubled.
I mothered Willie.
I loved Wilfred Blunt.

Grania: That is better.
You have spoken the name.

Lady Gregory: I have spoken his name.
Is that what you wanted
To force me to do?
Very well. I speak it.

I loved Wilfred Scawen Blunt
With all the power
Of a woman's heart to love.

Grania: Go on.

Lady Gregory: It was two years into my marriage
And we were in Egypt
Where my husband had taken me
To curtail my involvement
With Robert and the nursery.
A too-young wife was embarrassment enough,
And an infant son too much.
So there I was in Egypt
Appendage to this aging man,
And two days after our arrival
I saw, standing across a room,
This young god.
Oh, can't you understand!

(DANCERS *enter upstage. Female, young* LADY GREGORY, *from R;* BLUNT
from L. BLUNT *strikes a pose. They dance, accompanied by plaintive
music. Meanwhile the dialog continues. Twice during the scene,
however, both the dance and the music are suspended, frozen and held
while* GRANIA *quotes sonnet lines and the dialogue briefly concerns
them. Each sonnet quote, here, as elsewhere in the play, is
accompanied by the soft chime that accompanied Grania's entrance at
the start of the play.)*

Grania: But I do.
He had the love spot on his forehead
As Diarmuid did.
Once you saw it,
You were lost.

Lady Gregory: Completely lost.
Oh, I saw no love spot
Only a wide brow,
Upswept chestnut hair,
Passionate brown eyes.
But I was as lost as you were
When Diarmuid's cap fell
And you saw the love spot on his brow.
There was no retreat.
All that I believed
Of duty to husband and child
Seemed to drain from me.

Grania: You wooed him
As I wooed Diarmuid?

Lady Gregory: I wooed him shamelessly.

Grania: 'The crime of having loved you yet unwooed
The guiltiness all mine alone.'

Lady Gregory: *(sharply)*
Why did you say that!

Grania: For no reason
The words just came to me.

(LADY GREGORY *continues to regard her sharply for a moment, then*
decides to continue. The music and dance resume.)

Lady Gregory: Yes, I wooed him shamelessly

I did not know I had such wiles.
To draw to me, to ensnare
This poet,
This lover of beautiful women.
And I not beautiful or famous,
I meek and small and plain
Drew this god into my bed,
Devising spots
Where we might meet alone
And lie in each other's arms.

I knew it was wicked, sinful,
And I could not care.
Knew even that it could not last,
That he would move on
As he did.

When he went off to India
I wrote 12 sonnets
Of our love.
I who had never written a poem
Wrote this poet sonnets.

(Music and dance freeze for sonnet quote and exchange about it.)

Grania: 'Wild words I write, wild words of
                      love and pain...'

Lady Gregory: What!

Grania: It is nothing. Go on.

(A bit disconcerted, but continues and music and dance unfreeze.)

Lady Gregory: I wrote this poet sonnets
                  And in the morning
                  After our last night together
                  I pressed them into his hand
                  To be read once
                  And then to be destroyed forever.
                  The only copy.
                  Then I went back to my husband.

(Dance over; dancers exit; dance music stops and chime accompanies sonnet quote.)

Grania: 'For me the light is dimmed, the dream
                      has past
                  I seek not gladness, yet may find content
                  Fulfilling each small duty, reach at last
                  Some goal of peace before my youth
                      is spent.'

Lady Gregory: You are doing it again.
                  Those lines were not in my play.
                  Why are you speaking those lines?

Grania: Who knows why. They came to me.
                  Stranger things have happened
                  On this mountain top.
                  You were saying you went back to
                      your husband.

Lady Gregory: Yes. I went back to my husband.

Grania:	And slept with him.
Lady Gregory:	When I could not avoid it.
	His health was uncertain
	And I played on his fears
	Of the ridicule
	More births might evoke.
	Pled that there be no more children.
Grania:	And there were not.
Lady Gregory:	No.
	So you see, Grania,
	I was too like you.
	Married to an old man,
	Wooing and loving a young one.
	But returning to her old husband.
	But the break was never a clean one.
	He went to India, yes.
	But he returned
	And for 40 years
	Until his death,
	Some years before my own,
	We kept in touch
	Like strangers or acquaintances only
	But in formal touch:
	Dear Mr. Blunt
	My dear Lady Gregory.

He called us friends for 40 years
Though how could we be friends
After what had passed between us?
Nights I could never forget
No matter how my conscience
Plagued me to put them down.

Friendship he called it.
Never once did he imply
That there had been
Anything more between us.

As 'friend' each year
He sent my grandchildren
A great Christmas tree
For the drawing room at Coole.

As 'friend' he willed me
His prison bible
Relic of a short
Incarceration in Ireland.

As 'friend'
I was summoned to his Sussex estate
In his last days
When pushed about in a bath chair
By his latest mistress
He fretted over his lack of poetic fame
And had the insensitivity

To ask me to read the diaries
He was publishing
As a final grasp
On the literary fame
He so coveted.

In 'friendship',
He even begged me
To write the preface
And in love, for fallen majesty perhaps,
I wrote it
Though I had found the diaries
At times dull
At other times
Full of hurtful anecdotes.

But perhaps asking me to read them
Was his way of tacitly assuring me
That no mention of our brief affair
Was in them.

Grania: You're sure of that?

Lady Gregory: I read every word.
                  I am mentioned only tangentially
                  As a friend.
                  He even said a few kind words
                  About my talent and tenacity.
                  Little did he understand
                  Anything about my talent and tenacity.

How all those years
To hide my hurt
I threw myself into any work
That came to hand
To help forget
To suppress the longing
That never ceased to throb.

With Yeats I helped found the Abbey,
Toiled for it incessantly,
Wrote little folk plays
To amuse the masses
Who could not understand
Yeats' beautiful poetic ones.
I did anything to keep the seats filled
Anything that came to hand.
Shaw called me
' The charwoman of the Abbey'

Grania: Did it never occur to you
                   That perhaps you had talents
                   More worthy than being
                   The charwoman of the Abbey?

Lady Gregory: Shaw meant that as a compliment.

Grania: Yes and no.
                   You abase yourself too much.

Lady Gregory: I never abase myself

I worked for our dream of Ireland
Worthy work
That needed to be doing.
I took the players on American tours,
I begged subscriptions
From the landed gentry,
Withstood the riots
Over the plays of Synge and O'Casey
Even when at times.
I disliked the plays themselves
But knew them good for our theatre,
Knew the very riots they evoked
Helped spread the Abbey's fame.

I even introduced Yeats to Wilfred,
Got Wilfred to write a verse play
For us.
Not a very good play, I'm afraid,
For I gradually realized,
Admitted to myself,
Wilfred Scawen Blunt was not a great poet
Though that did not stop my loving him.

Grania: You are rambling off the track.
                     This does not answer my question.

Lady Gregory: I am perhaps trying to understand
                     My own motives
                     So that I can answer your question.
                     Why did I write Grania

	And then suppress it? That is what you want to know. I am trying to tell you.
Grania:	But you go roundabout. Why did you write it?
Lady Gregory:	Because I had to! I was 60 years old. For 30 years that brief affair Had tortured me With loss With regret With remorse And with chagrin, That never, though I saw Wilfred's faults, And they were many, Could I stop loving him. I saw too that out of my strength In leaving him, Of putting off my love for duty, I had made a life. Perhaps not of my choosing But a life. I had had to forget Or try to. I had thrown my passion Into the theatre, Later into the fruitless effort

To recapture Hugh Lane's pictures
For Ireland
After he tragically drowned
On the *Luisitania*
Leaving an ambiguous will
That seemed to leave
Those magnificent French
  Impressionist paintings
To London, not to Ireland
As I knew he intended.

Grania: This is temporizing
Your nephew Hugh Lane's paintings
Have nothing to do with what I have
  asked you.
Why must you rehearse your biography
And avoid a direct answer?

Lady Gregory: I am trying to answer you.
I am trying to understand myself.
There I was
30 years after the event
Still smarting
But holding my head high.

Perhaps I wrote for Wilfred
To show him I did not care
That like Grania
I could renounce love
Be strong
Move on.

Grania: But surely he could have seen that
                    And you living your life as you did.

Lady Gregory: Perhaps you are right.
                    So perhaps it was for a different reason.
                    Perhaps I wanted the story of my love,
                    The pain of my renunciation recorded.

                    Perhaps I wrote it at first
                    Only for myself.
                    But when I had written it
                    I wanted Wilfred to read it.
                    Yes, I wanted him to be hurt by it.
                    So I let it be printed
                    Saw that he had a copy.

Grania: And did it hurt him?

Lady Gregory: I doubt it.
                    We never discussed it.
                    No, that ploy failed.
                    And then I panicked
                    At my own audacity,
                    Felt that should the play be staged,
                    The passions
                    And their correspondence
                    To my own life
                    Might shine through
                    And the underlying story be revealed.

(Chime for quote)

Grania: 'Should e'er that drear day come in
                       which the world
                   Shall know the secret which so close I hold,
                   Should taunts and jeers at my bowed
                       head be hurled
                   And all my love and all my shame be told...

                   I could not, knowing all the story true
                   Hold up my head and brave the talk
                       of town....'

Lady Gregory: Stop that!
                   You are crooning words you should
                       not know.

Grania: I cannot help it.
                   Suddenly I find them on my tongue.
                   It is strange, is it not
                   How words once loosed
                   Can echo down the years?
                   I did not realize
                   I was about to speak them.
                   It was as though a greater power
                   Forced them from my lips.

                   Forgive me.
                   Go on.

Lady Gregory: Your words have troubled me.
                 They should not have been in your mouth.
                 They should not echo on this mountain top.

Grania: I have upset you.
                 I am sorry.

Lady Gregory: You have not upset me.
                 Mere girl that you are
                 You have no power to upset me!
                 But you keep reciting lines of banal verse
                 That seem half familiar
                 But have nothing to do with my story.
                 Try to keep silent
                 Let me finish
                 And leave this mountain top
                 To its circling daws.

Grania: Go on.

Lady Gregory: And do not speak to me
                 In that imperious tone
                 I will not accept it.
                 Do you understand?

Grania: Perhaps I understand
                 More than you realize
                 But I will be still.
                 Continue as you will.

Lady Gregory: You have broken my thread of thought.
                 Where was I?

Grania: You feared your own story might
                    shine through.

Lady Gregory: Ah yes, I did fear it.

                 But I did want it on record
                 Disguised, but on record
                 The story of my only real love.

                 You see except in my heart
                 There was no record of it
                 Only in my heart
                 And in the sonnets
                 And of them
                 There had been only the one copy
                 In my own hand
                 And that burned

Grania: You were wrong

Lady Gregory: To suppress the play
                 To deny you your moment of glory?

Grania: To forbid the play.
                 It might have been safer then than now.

Lady Gregory: I don't understand what you mean.

Grania: Well, you counted too much
                 On the man's discretion.
                 He did not burn your sonnets.

Lady Gregory: He swore he did.

Grania: He lied.
                 He did not burn them,
                 Nor your love letters
                 All in your own hand.

Lady Gregory: This cannot be true.

Grania: It is true. They are there.
                 Among his private papers
                 His diaries.

Lady Gregory: But you are wrong.
                 You have not been listening.
                 I read his diaries
                 They were published;
                 For me they contained no harm.

Grania: You read his published diaries
                 The ones he wanted you to read
                 But there were secret diaries
                 Willed to the library at Cambridge
                 To be opened long after his death.

                 And 40 years after he died,

They were opened
And quickly closed again.
But your story is there
Along with your sonnets

(Chime for sonnet quote; then Grania continues.)

'And I have learned in love lore to be wise
And knowledge of the evil and the good
Have had one moment's glimpse of paradise
And know the flavor of forbidden food...'

Shall I go on? I can.
They are your own words.
From your sonnets.

Lady Gregory: Now I begin to undersand your game.
You have somehow plucked lines
From those long forgotten sonnets.
But that is impossible.
Even I cannot remember them exactly.
I wrote them in the heat of passion
The night before we parted.
The next morning I pressed the only copy
Into his hand.
He swore he burned them.
I cannot believe he did not.
Some power I do not understand
Has whirled those words into your head.
That this mountain is bewitched
Is hard for me to believe

But easier than to believe
He kept the sonnets
Or that he kept secret diaries.

Grania: Come now, didn't you as well
                 Confide in your journals
                 Memories of your secret heart?
                 Of course you did.
                 But you had the grace, the decency
                 To edit and destroy.
                 You tidied up your journals
                 Before your death
                 Knowing well they would be published
                 And careful as always
                 To hurt no one.

Lady Gregory: Despite your uncanny knowledge
                 I cannot believe you.
                 I burned all.
                 He promised to as well.

Grania: Men often make promises they fail to keep.

Lady Gregory: No. No. There must be some mistake.

Grania: No mistake.
                 Women are fools to trust a man's love.
                 In your heart you always knew that,
                 Knew your love for him
                 Was deeper than his love for you.

He kept your letters
And the poems,
Manuscripts in your own hand.
And as he, from a distance,
Saw your fame grow great
Perhaps greater than posterity
Would grant to him,
He made sure not to destroy them.

You cringed in guilt
Fearing your secret might out.
Could that have been so dire?
Was it important enough
To deny the power of your own voice
Speaking through me?

Was it not important that having
    written words
Worthy for Grania's lips to speak
Worthy because they were woman's words
Coming from a woman's heart
That they should be spoken?

You strangled those words.
You put a bandage about my mouth
You forbid my speaking them.

And is it not important
That in doing so
You strangled yourself as well

Denied your own gifts
Cowered behind a mask of respectability
You felt you must preserve for the world?

Oh, others had written plays of Grania
Given me lines to speak on other stages
But those others had been men
Who could not know the passions
In Grania's heart.
You knew those passions.

> *It is for you I will wear my jewels*
> *And my golden dress*
> *For you are my share of life*
> *And you are the east and the west to me*
> *And all the long ago*
> *And all that is before me*

You gave me those words of love for
   Diarmuid.
And you gave me words of hurt and
   loss and anger
When he abandoned me.

> *He had no love for me at any time*
> *It is easy to know that now.*
> *I knew it all the while*
> *But would not give in to believe it.*
> *...were I to die*
> *With this scald on my heart*

It is hard thistles would spring up
Out of my grave.
(For) it is women are said to change
And they do not.
But it is men that change and turn
As often as the wheel of the moon.

Admit it . These are your words.
Stronger than those that forgotten
   poet ever wrote.

Admit it.
The name of Lady Augusta Gregory
Is known to all the world
While only a few scholars
Remember the poet Wilfred Scawen Blunt.

Oh, you wrote better than you knew
When you wrote your play about me.
Diarmuid in the end betrayed me,
Loved his allegiance to Finn
More than he loved Grania.
And in your heart
You know Wilfred Blunt
Always loved his roles of poet
And political rebel
More than he loved any woman
Including you.

He saved your letters

Because they assure him
Of at least a footnote
In a history more illustrious
Than his own.
Can't you see that?

Lady Gregory: The letters, the sonnets?
In my own hand.
You are sure?

Grania: I am sure
But buried at Cambridge.
Few scholars have unearthed them
But among those few your secret is out,
More blatantly than the play
You suppressed would have risked.

Lady Gregory: It is well that I am sitting
For my head reels.
You might, Grania,
Have told me this sooner
Without your dragging from me
A secret you already knew,
Without your fretting me
With snatches from those sonnets
And words I had half forgotten.
You have been toying with me this night
And that is unkind.
You are a hard woman, Grania,
And the bargain you drive, a hard one.

Grania: You knew of my hardness.
It was that
Not Deirdre's pliancy
That drew you to my story.
And it is in your play
That my hardness shines through.

Lady Gregory: It does.
Ah well, I suppose it no longer matters.
When I wrote those sonnets
The world would have judged me a
    wicked woman
Though never would have felt Wilfred a
    wicked man.
But in the modern world,
Grania, which neither you nor I inhabited
Women may now fare better
Be judged as the men are judged
Forgiven as they are forgiven.
It is all one can hope for.

I am known in the book of the people
For other matters
And little they may care
So long a time having passed
That in my youth
I too was a foolish woman
Who trusted where I should not.

It is a hard thing, Grania,

To renounce one you trusted
But now I do.
And you are right, Grania,
In my play
I wrote far better than I knew
For who would have thought
He loved fame
Or fancied fame
More than he, if not, loved
At least respected, me?

Yes, I wrote better than I knew
When I had you renounce Diarmuid
And your love for him
And walk away with your head held high
And wearing your jewels and your
  golden dress.

Grania:
    And I have lost
    All this side of the world
    Losing that trust and faith I had
    And finding him to think of me
    No more than a flock of stares
    Would cast a shadow on his path.

    So...You give me leave?
    You will let me speak those lines?

Lady Gregory: I give you leave.
    It may be too late

And the world may no longer care
To hear them
But I give you leave.
I give you your voice, Grania,
May you shout the words
From all the world's stages.

> *For there is not since an hour ago*
> *Any sound that would matter at all*
> *Or be more to me*
> *Than the screaming of wild geese*
>   *overhead.*

Go, Grania.
I think we are free of each other at last.

(GRANIA hesistates, makes to embrace LADY GREGORY, but something in the lofty pride mades her hesitate....She stands a moment....then exits L.)

Lady Gregory: It is well I brought my jewels
And my golden dress.

(She rather defiantly discards her stick, leaning it against the"rock" on which she has been sitting, hangs her veiled hat on it and exits R, down the mountain walking firmly with her head held high.)

Second: And that is it?

First: Isn't it enough?

Second: But something should be changed.

First: It has been.

In her other plays
Lady Gregory was writing
The Book of the People.
In Grania, she wrote
The book of herself.
She has finally given it her blessing.

Second: But who won? Grania?

First: It is not about winning or losing.
But perhaps your answer to that
Is even now on the path.

(Young shepherd BOY *enters, climbing from R.)*

Boy: Did you see a stray lamb
And it caught in a bush?

First: I did not.
But did you see an old woman on the path
As you climbed up?

Boy: I did not.
But I saw a young girl
And she had the walk of a queen.

*(*FIRST MUSICIAN *nods to* SECOND *and they begin to play. The young* BOY *catches the spirit and dances happily -- jig or step dance steps. Then playing happily the musicians and boy exit down the aisle, off the mountain and end the play.)*

(Lights dim.)

(Notes: Probably most of the audience will not notice that the ending lines are deliberately lifted from Cathleen ni Houlihan. Among those who do, most will believe Yeats wrote them; a few may know that Lady Gregory who helped him "Irish" his peasant dialogue, probably wrote them; and a very few may know that the only time Lady Gregory ever acted on a stage, in her old age she once played the role that Yeats had written so many years ago for Maud Gonne. None of this matters but it is nice to have in the background.)

Ezra's Noh
for Willie

EZRA'S NOH FOR WILLIE was first presented in the Welles
Gallery of the Lenox Library, Lenox, Massachusetts, on March
1, 1990, with the following cast:

Ezra Pound . . . . Spenser Trova
Sean MacBride . . . . David Raskin
Lady Gregory . . . . Meeghan Holoway
Cuchulain . . . . Glenn Barrett
The Grey Macha . . . . Jane Goodrich
Loeg . . . . Bruce Macdonald
First Musician . . . . Leigh Nelson (drone)
Second Musician . . . . Sushil Mukherjee (flute)
Third Musician . . . . Terrence Hall (drums)
Direction . . . . Frances Benn Hall

The first production of EZRA'S NOH FOR WILLIE
in Ireland was presented by the Delphic Players
of Belfast in Clifton, Connemara, Galway, on July 7, 1995
with the following cast:

Ezra Pound . . . . Zelda Clegg
Sean Macbride . . . . Jim Gibson
Lady Gregory . . . . Claire Connell
Georgie Yeats . . . . Roisin Gibson
Cuchulain . . . . Martin Mc Ilroy
Grey Macha . . . . Clare Mc Cusker
Loeg . . . . Thomas Muinzer
Chorus/Musician . . . . Andrew Blackwell
Original Music . . . . Ursula Burns
Director . . . . Louis Muinzer

Ezra's Noh for Willie

<pre>
Characters: Ezra Pound
               Lady Gregory
               Sean MacBride
               Georgie Yeats
               Cuchulain
               The Grey Macha,
                 horse/dancer
               Loeg
               Three musicians
                 (bamboo flute, drone, drum)
</pre>

(Stage bare except for Ezra's cage, free-standing bamboo that can be easily struck. Mythic characters are costumed and masked; Musicians *in black; "real" characters in real clothes.)*

(Lights up on Ezra *in his cage.)*

Ezra:
I stand in my cage in the hot sun.
They call me mad.
I am locked up
But still they are afraid.
Soldiers with guns guard me.
I have no gun
But finally they have given me
Paper--and a pen
And so, in my Pisa cage,
I can sit and write about Willie.
And because the pen rules time,
I can summon all time,

Past and passing and to come,
Can sing like Willie
Golden bird--not on a bough
But in a cage.

And so for Willie, I have made a play
It is a Noh play, a spirit play.
Willie trafficked in spirits.
In spirit plays everyone is dead.
That is as it should be.
Everyone in this play is dead.
Even I, though I seem to speak
To you from my cage, am long dead.
Only the vision of the cage remains.
Only the vision
Of those in my play remains.
But all comes round again on the wheel.
Listen then to a spirit play for Willie.

(MUSICIANS *enter after first speech. Sit on floor DL. They accompany dance and at times take lines.)*

First Musician: The gyres spin
                    And out of myth is myth again reborn.
                    Here in the harbor, the Macha
                    Paws the waves of Galway Bay
                    And circling seabirds
                    Cut arcs above her masts,
                    As once more the Grey Macha
                    Bears Cuchulain home.

Lady Gregory: *(enters from audience)*
                  Long dead and Coole torn down
                  But my park nearby
                  I come in unseen tribute
                  To stand on the quay
                  Having given him the mask
                  He wore so long
                  Until Cuchulain's face
                  Became his own,
                  Until he came to be at last
                  The hero he longed to be.
                  And yet that it should be the Macha
                  Cuchulain's Grey Macha
                  That bears him home
                  Seems almost more
                  Than soul can hope.

Ezra: Don't be too sure.
                  Willie worked everything out.
                  I saw it at Rapello,
                  Playing the wicked old man
                  But planning it all--
                  Drumcliff and the cold eye.
                  He wove his life like a tapestry,
                  Only grieved when he couldn't get
                  The thread he wanted.
                  There was one woman....

Sean Macbride: *(enters from audience DR)*
                  My mother--

And so by a trick of whirling gyres
I, only son of that woman
He loved so many years,
But who was never moved
By references to Helen
And the counting of swans,
That woman, my mother,
Outlived him long
Yet has not journeyed
To this quayside
Here in Galway Bay.
But I, by whirl of gyres
Minister of External Affairs
For Ireland,
Stand here, representing
Not my mother, but my country,
There's irony in that.
And yet he loved my mother.
Asked her again and again
To marry him.
But she would only laugh and say
'Willie, the world should thank me
For not marrying you.
Think of all the poems.'

Georgie: *(appearing from audience)*
Or thank me for marrying him.
Giving him the son and daughter
He begged the Old Fathers
To pardon him for not having.

I gave him Anne and Michael
And I gave him much more.
I dreamed the Vision
That he paced into poems
On the battlement.
The gyres perne
Because together we found them.

Ezra: And yet for all his planning,
               His careful calculations,
               Surely he could not have
               Foreseen it would be the Macha.

Georgie: Not foreseen!
               I say he foresaw all.
               Do you think it chance,
               Mere chance,
               That when his book of life,
               His poems,
               Came full circle,
               As he knew they would,
               The pivot, 'The Second Coming',
               Is number 200?
               Do you think that
               Sleepless in his tower
               Ordering his poems' order,
               He would not have foreseen,
               Or perhaps foresaw,
               Not knowing he foresaw?
               The gyres spin

	And time is only time
	Come round again on the wheel.
	But it was my dream hand
	That gave him the wheel,
	The gyres, the vision.
	The world should well thank me
	For marrying him.
Ezra:	Ladies, for Maud speaks in Sean,
	Ladies, we are all dead
	In the moon's dark.
	It is useless to praise or blame.
	Let us rejoice rather
	That it is the Macha
	That brings him home,
	And in honor of that Macha
	Stop now
	Leave the stage to the musicians
	And my play--
	Ezra's Noh for Willie.

(Blackout; all characters leave stage; cage struck; lights up on musicians.)

First Musician:	I call to the eye of the mind
	A man grown tired and old
	Who would rest all day in his tent
	If a runner had not told
	That fighting now tore the plain
	And Cuchulain must seize his spear
	To rush into battle again
	With his horse and his charioteer.

Cuchulain: *(enters UR.)*
Loeg, Loeg, why do you tarry?
I bade you ready my battle car.

Loeg: *(enters L)*
I tried.
The Black Sainglenn stands
Quiet in harness
But the Grey Macha,
I swear by the gods
By which my people swear,
Though all the men
Of the Red Branch
Were around the Grey,
They could not bring him to chariot.
See, he comes, his eyes blazing
His mouth forming.

(The GREY MACHA, dancer, enters L. Dances, cutting great swooping circles around CUCHULAIN, each time coming to him but offering him his left side only, then shying away from him to dance and swoop again. Finally retreats DL and stands panting.)

Cuchulain: Come, my beauty.
Let me bind you to the chariot.
I know your fear,
It beats in my heart too,
And all the omens are mummy wound.
When I drew on my mantle,
This brooch fell and pierced my foot.
See, I limp,
But the battle rages again

And we cannot stay safe in the tents.
Come. I will yoke you with my own hands.

(Slowly the horse crosses UR to Cuchulain *and lays his head on Cuchulain's breast. Tableaux--to be repeated, with variation, at the play's end.)*

(Blackout. Actors leave stage. Lights up)

First Musician: Though he knows that the gyres have spun
Away with his luck and his pride,
He fights like an old man young
And will not be denied
A death standing on his feet
Though his blood is ebbing fast
And the wounded Grey comes to him
To lay a head on his breast.

*(*Cuchulain *staggers in UL trailing a blood red scarf from his belt. He crosses to pillar UR, which may be pantomimed, leans against it , fumblingly binding himself to it with one loop of the scarf.)*

(The Grey Macha *enters L, trailing a very long red scarf that should whip out behind as he dances. He circles the stage three times in great swoops that bind* Cuchulain *firmly to the pillar. Then the horse comes to him and lays his head on Cuchulain's breast. Cuchulain's head drops to rest on the head of the horse. SILENCE as the music comes to an abrupt halt. Both are perfectly still. Tableaux. Then the flute gives one long bird cry.)*

(Blackout. Actors off. Lights up on Ezra *in his cage.)*

Ezra: That's the play, mostly dance
As it should be.
But it must end with a song.

So the musicians will sing.

(MUSICIANS *shake their heads.*)

Ezra: No? They will not sing.
                         They think my bumpy rhymes will not skip.
                         Very well. The musicians will recite.

(MUSICIANS *again refuse.*)

Ezra: Very well, I will recite.
                         They will perhaps accompany me
                         If the spirit moves them.
                         That is almost a pun
                         In a Noh play.
                         I recite.
                         (mood changes)

                         He bade us fill the cradles right
                         But we have sorry skills compared
                         To those his muse or daemon might
                         Have withheld had he not cared
                         So deeply that he never spared
                         Himself or others any pain
                         That could become poetic gain.
                         That could help weave the cloak that he
                         Wore naked for the world to see.

                         His art, his life, his hopes, his fears,
                         Whirl in the gyres of his years.
                         Be it the Red Branch or the Rising

We have a poem of his devising.
Sligo's a shrine, the Tower a must,
Albert Power carved his bust,
While Abbey vies with Moscow Art
To see who'll play the longer part.

On this observance of his worth
Those who still have life and breath
Remember that til bitter end
He exhorted foe and friend
To be gay and keep on climbing
Up the mountainside of rhyming
And though he bids us with cold eye
Not to tarry, but pass by,
He lives his dream, a singing bird,
Golden throated, every word.

That's all Ezra has to say.
Thank you for coming to his play.

Note on author:

Frances Benn Hall's first play was produced at the University of Wisconsin where she received her Masters of Arts degree in Theatre. Since that time she has written many plays, been in playwriting seminars led by John Gassner, Harold Clurman, Sinclair Lewis, and William Gibson, and has furthered her theatre studies a UCLA, Trinity College Oxford, and at Yeats and Synge summer schools in Ireland where in 1995 she was playwright in residence at the Kiltartan Hedge School.

Recipient of grants from the National Endowment for the Arts and the Massachusetts Cultural Council, she lives, writes and produces plays in the Berkshires.